Dolphins

Voices in the Ocean

Dolphins

Voices in the Ocean

SUSAN CASEY

Delacorte Press

For Michael Casey and Sarah Casey,
with oceans of love

Text copyright © 2015, 2018 by Susan Casey
Jacket art by Neirfy/Shutterstock

This work is based on *Voices in the Ocean: A Journey into the Wild and Haunting World
of Dolphins*, copyright © 2015 by Susan Casey. Published in hardcover by Doubleday,
a division of Penguin Random House LLC, New York, in 2015.

Visit us on the Web! rhcbooks.com

Educators and librarians, for a variety of teaching tools,
visit us at RHTeachersLibrarians.com

Library of Congress Cataloging-in-Publication Data is available upon request.
ISBN 978-1-5247-0085-0 (HC) — ISBN 978-1-5247-0086-7 (lib. bdg.) —
ISBN 978-1-5247-0087-4 (ebook)

The text of this book is set in 12-point Adobe Caslon Pro.
Interior design by Jinna Shin

Printed in the United States of America
10 9 8 7 6 5 4 3 2 1
First Edition

Contents

≈≈≈≈

If there is magic on this planet,
it is contained in water.

—*Loren Eiseley*

Introduction

*A*ll the species I write about in these pages are toothed whales, one of two branches of cetaceans, a marine mammal group that includes whales, dolphins, and porpoises. The word "cetacean" comes from the Latin *cetus*, which means "whale," and the Greek *ketos*, with its rather less flattering translation: "sea monster."

Oceanic dolphins are the largest family of toothed whales, containing approximately thirty-seven species that range from the three-foot Hector's dolphin to the twelve-foot bottlenose dolphin to the twenty-five-foot orca, or killer whale. The oceanic dolphins also include pilot whales, melon-headed whales, false killer whales, and pygmy killer whales. Among this group, the word *whale* is used to indicate a creature's size (very big, or at least bigger than your average dolphin) rather than being a precise scientific description.

However, not all dolphins live in the ocean. There are five species of river dolphins—the Iniidae—remarkable, prehistoric-looking animals like the Amazon boto, the Ganges River dolphin, and the now-extinct baiji, formerly found in China's Yangtze River.

Porpoises are a separate group entirely. The seven species of porpoises, or Phocoenidae, are smaller, and distinct from dolphins.

Chapter 1

Honolua

~~~~~~

To get to Hawaii from anywhere in the world, you must fly for at least six hours across the Pacific Ocean. If you look out the window during that time, you will see only water below you, and maybe a few clouds. Though they are officially part of the United States—the fiftieth state, to be exact—the Hawaiian Islands are the most remote lands on Earth, surrounded in all directions by thousands of miles of salt water. Which was exactly why I wanted to be there.

I'd flown to the island of Maui to escape everything in my life. I wanted to run as far as possible from my apartment in New York City, from the concrete and gray skies and traffic and breathless crush of Manhattan. Most of all, I was hoping to escape my feelings of sadness.

1

Two years earlier, my father had died suddenly of a heart attack, and since then, sorrow had followed me around like a dark fog. Dad's death took our family totally by surprise. He was seventy-one years old and athletic and strong, and he had collapsed at our summer cottage, walking down to the lake. I still couldn't believe he was really gone.

In some far corner of my mind, I had always known, as every person does, that my father wouldn't be around forever, but the idea of losing him was so big and overwhelming that I never gave it any space. He had inspired me to roam the world making mistakes and having adventures; he had urged me to follow my dreams and to believe in myself. "You can do *anything* you put your mind to," he'd told me. Through years of ups and downs, joys and frustrations, my father was the person I'd always counted on for support, encouragement, confidence, love. Whatever happened, I could trust he'd be there to help me make sense of it. Only now, he wasn't.

Everybody copes with grief in their own way. Some people turn to family and friends. Others take comfort in spiritual beliefs, or in the peace and beauty of nature. The one thing that has always made me feel better is swimming. Being in any body of water is soothing to me, but I especially love to swim in the ocean. So on my last day on Maui, I'd driven across the island to visit Honolua Bay, a spot that Native Hawaiians had long held sacred. The bay was postcard-pretty but also rugged: it was surrounded by steep cliffs and ringed with a rocky shoreline. There were no soft sand beaches here.

I drove up a steep red-dirt road and pulled over at the top. Usually this lookout was crowded, but on this day the weather was dreary and no one else was around. I got out and walked to the edge of the embankment. Below me waves crashed, their crests whipped white by the wind. Rain clouds pressed down, turning the turquoise water a dull navy color.

Conditions were crummy, but this particular bay was known for its beauty, its lush coral reefs and colorful fish, so I didn't want to leave without at least taking a dip. I wouldn't have another chance to swim here for a long time: the following day I would be on a plane flying home.

But there was a problem, and it was more than the weather. I'd read in the local newspaper that a recent flurry of shark attacks here had people thinking twice about going into the water alone, or even at all. Swimmers and surfers wondered nervously why the sharks seemed so hungry, but no one had any answers. I stood in the wind thinking about this, and after a few moments spent listening to my mind spin tales of lost limbs, severed arteries, nothing left of me but a few scraps of bathing suit, I picked my way down the path and across the rocks, stepped into the shallows, and began to swim.

The water was dark and kind of spooky at first, but that didn't stop me. Since my dad's death I'd felt numb, as though I were sleepwalking. What could be worse than life without the person I loved most? Tiger sharks seemed like a minor concern.

As I headed across the mouth of the bay I veered out to sea, until I was a half mile offshore. Treading water, I cleared my goggles and looked around. The visibility was good, better than expected. I could see all the way down to the seafloor, and conditions were smoother out here, so I kept swimming.

Ten minutes later, I was about to turn back to shore when a movement caught my eye: a large gray body passed below me. Then a dorsal fin broke the surface. Streaks of sunlight broke through the clouds, and suddenly the water was illuminated. My heart raced as the creatures revealed themselves.

It was a pod of spinner dolphins, forty or fifty animals, swimming toward me. They emerged from the ocean like ghosts, shimmering in the water. One moment they were barely visible, then they were gone, and then they reappeared on all sides, surrounding me.

I had never been this close to dolphins before, and I

was amazed by their appearance. One of the bigger spinners approached slowly, watching me. For a moment we hung there and looked at one another, exchanging what I can only describe as a greeting. His eyes were banded delicately with black, markings that trailed to his pectoral fins like a bank robber's mask. I wondered if he was the pod's guardian, if the others followed his lead. The dolphins were traveling in small clusters of two and three, and they maintained close body contact. I saw fins touching, bellies brushing across backs, heads tilted toward other heads, beaks slipped under flukes.

The entire pod could have darted away in an instant, but they chose instead to stay with me. Spinners are known for their athletics, leaping out of the water whenever the urge strikes, but these dolphins were relaxed. They showed no fear even though they were traveling with several baby spinners, calves the size of bowling pins tucked in beside their mothers. The dolphins had simply enfolded me in their gathering, and I could hear their clicks and buzzes underwater, their aquatic conversation.

I dove down and the big dolphin appeared beside me again, even closer. He had markings like a penguin's, dark on top and white on his belly, with a slender beak. At six feet long he was a powerful animal, but nothing in his body language suggested hostility. We stayed together for only a few minutes, but the time stretched like taffy. The ocean rose and fell in a soft rhythm, and below the surface everything was bathed in a blue glow. The dolphins watched me watching them. I swam with the spinners until they headed into deeper waters, where light dropped off to nowhere in long, slanting rays. The last thing I saw before they vanished back into their world was their tails, moving in unison.

≈≈≈≈≈≈

After my encounter with them, I thought of the dolphins often. Not just for hours or days afterward, but for weeks and months. I thought of them at night as I was going to sleep—remembering their languid swimming motions made me feel relaxed and drowsy and calm. I thought of the dolphins after I left Hawaii and returned to Manhattan, where life was anything but relaxed and drowsy and calm, and where the luminous blues of the Pacific Ocean were a distant memory. In the office where I worked as a magazine editor, on the thirty-sixth floor of a towering glass-and-steel skyscraper, I thumbtacked dolphin pictures above my desk so I could look at them while I made phone calls.

However brief, my dolphin visitation was stuck inside

my head. It was as though I'd been hit by lightning and that one strike had zapped clean through my brain, replacing its usual patterns and wavelengths with a dolphin highlight reel. I couldn't forget the way the pod had sized me up, or their peculiar squeaking, creaking language, or how ridiculously *fun* it was to cruise along with them. I could tell there was somebody home behind each set of eyes, and I wanted to know more about who they were. I'd met other intriguing sea creatures, some shy and some bold, some beautiful and some that only Mother Nature could love, but none of them had the same presence as the dolphins—not the puffer fish that looked like tiny Buddhas, or the spotted eagle rays that resembled spaceships, or the sea turtles with their ancient, armored shells and wise faces.

But as I thought about the dolphins, my strongest memory was how *otherworldly* they were. As the spinners swam by, they seemed to exist in a more exotic realm than our own. They inhabited what Aboriginal Australian people called the Dreamtime, a gauzy, blissful place located somewhere between reality and imagination.

Certainly, dolphins can do many things that seem almost magical. They can see with their hearing, deploying high-frequency sonar to effectively produce X-ray vision. This ability, called echolocation, means that dolphins can literally see through objects. Using their sonar, they can tell—even in the dark—if another dolphin (or a human being) is pregnant or sick or injured. A dolphin's sonar is much more advanced than a nuclear submarine's; scientists suspect that dolphins can even use their echolocation skills to determine another creature's emotional state. Dolphins can communicate at far higher frequencies than we can hear, and navigate electrical and magnetic fields that are imperceptible to us. They can stay awake and alert for fifteen days straight.

Surprisingly, dolphins didn't always live in the water. Their earliest ancestors, ninety-five million years ago, were land mammals that resembled small, hooved wolves. After living for a while in swamps and coastal lowlands, these fledgling aquanauts moved permanently into the water. Over the course of twenty million years (give or take a million or two), their limbs turned to fins, their shape became streamlined for swimming, their fur turned to blubber, and their nostrils migrated to the top of their heads and became blowholes—they developed all the equipment they needed to master undersea life. Dolphins' bodies are so perfectly adapted for speed, navigation, diving into the depths, and keeping warm that it's hard to imagine improvements.

But while it's tempting to project onto dolphins all the superpowers we wish we had ourselves, in truth they are creatures who, like us, can feel cranky or frustrated or have their own version of a bad day. Dolphins don't always act like angels; their range of less-than-cuddly behaviors is just as wide as ours. In fact, despite the big differences between our two species, possibly the most surprising thing about dolphins is just how much they resemble *us*.

In any pod you'll find all kinds of little groups, dolphins hanging out in duos and trios and quartets, mothers and babies and aunts, playful teenagers, flirty couples, wily hunters, wise elders—and their associations are anything but random. Dolphins are very social creatures. They're also chatterboxes who recognize themselves in the mirror, count, cheer, giggle, feel sad, stroke each other, adorn themselves, use tools, make jokes, enjoy music, bring presents on a date, introduce themselves, rescue one another from dangerous situations, manipulate, improvise, form tight bonds, throw tantrums, gossip, scheme, grieve, comfort, anticipate, fear, and love—just like we do.

The Hawaiian dolphins were like an ancient tribe I had stumbled upon, and though I didn't understand their language, they had somehow communicated with me. More important, for reasons I could not put into words, the spinners made me feel better. They took the edge off my sadness. During the moments I revisited them in my mind, the dolphins made me feel happy again.

Once I started paying attention to dolphins, I began to notice them everywhere. They were often in the news, and extremely popular on the Internet. I read stories about dolphins helping salvagers find lost undersea treasure, dolphins saving surfers from shark attacks, dolphins recruited as soldiers by the US Navy. While scientists argued about whether animals could possibly have their own cultures and customs, dolphins and their close relatives—whales—were observed making babysitting arrangements, gathering for a funeral, and calling one another by name. A group of marine biologists reported that after seven years in captivity a beluga whale named Noc had started to communicate with his trainers—in English. Belugas, members of the toothed whale family along with dolphins, have been nicknamed "the canaries of the sea" for their expressive vocals. Among other things, Noc had told a diver to get out of his tank. The whale had been insistent, the biologists said: "Our observations led us to conclude the 'out' which was repeated several times came from Noc."

We've known for a long time now that dolphin brains are impressive, bigger even than human brains. Yet scientists still don't know what the dolphins are doing with such heavy-duty machinery (or, for that matter, what human brains are really up to). To run a big brain takes a lot of energy; neither humans nor dolphins would possess such a powerful engine if it weren't in some way essential for their survival. A clue emerged when dolphin brains, like ours, were found to contain special, turbocharged neurons that relate to empathy, intuition, socializing, and self-awareness. Interestingly, dolphins have three times more of these neurons than we do, and they are thought to have developed them 30 million years ago, about 29.8 million years before our ancestors did.

While scientists made news with their dolphin findings, the animals also caught the attention of the film world. *The Cove,* a movie about a cruel dolphin hunt in Taiji, Japan, riveted audiences and won the Oscar for Best Documentary in 2010. The movie revealed how each year local fishermen conduct this hunt, driving entire pods of dolphins into a narrow cove, then blocking off the entrance and killing them with knives and spears. The fishermen's goal is to get rid of as many dolphins as possible because they resent the animals for eating fish that could otherwise be eaten by humans.

Most of the captured dolphins end up in Japanese supermarkets and restaurants (though the meat is highly contaminated with mercury and other toxins), but some do not. Younger females and calves are separated out, examined by trainers and dolphin brokers, and then sold to marine parks for hundreds of thousands of dollars. Every year, the hunters kill or sell hundreds of dolphins.

But sadly, Japan isn't the only place dolphins are dying in large numbers: they are washing up on shores all over the world. Scientists have searched to understand why this is happening, but pinning down a single problem is hard—there are so many. In California, dolphins are suffering from skin wounds and infections. In Florida, dolphins are dying from cancer. Across Europe, dolphins have washed up thin and starving. Everywhere in the world, dolphins have been so poisoned by pollution—pesticides, heavy metals, toxic chemicals—that their bodies are disposed of as hazardous waste. On top of this, the dolphins, with their extra-sensitive hearing, suffer due to rising levels of man-made underwater noise: drilling, ship engines, oil rig construction, explosives, and military sonar that can blast sound across entire ocean basins. These extremely loud sounds harass millions of animals and can even kill them. "The future for dolphins is a lot gloomier than their smiling faces suggest," an article in *New Scientist* detailed.

If reading about these problems makes you upset, you are not alone. It's not just the idea of dolphins in trouble—dolphins in general strike a deep emotional chord in most people. On some level, we seem to know how connected we are, the dolphins and us, and how we share the same fate.

Scientists reject the idea that dolphins stir our emotions because we have a built-in spiritual connection to them, but that doesn't make us feel it any less. Anyone who's ever spent time around a dolphin, any dolphin, faces thought-provoking questions such as these posed by marine biologist Rachel Smolker: "Do [dolphins] have the same powers of reasoning that we have? Are they self-aware? Do they feel love and hate, compassion, trust, distrust? Do they wonder about death? Do they have ideas about right and wrong? What could they teach us about the oceans? How do they feel about one another? What do they think about us?"

What *is* it about dolphins? Even far back in history, there are stories of the unique bond between our species. The Greeks and Romans, the early Europeans, the Maoris and Aboriginal Australians and Amazon tribes and Pacific Islanders—they were all dolphin crazy. Actually, everyone was. Dolphins were painted on palace walls, sculpted into statues, stamped on gold coins, tattooed onto bodies. In ancient Greece, it is said, dolphins had the same rights as people: to kill a dolphin was equal to murder. Our relationship with dolphins might even have included literal conversation. In 350 BC, the philosopher Aristotle wrote:

"The voice of the dolphin in air is like that of the human in that they can pronounce vowels and combinations of vowels, but have trouble with the consonants."

The idea of a dolphin poking his head above the water to speak to us is like something out of a dream. It is true that dolphins have the brainpower and the communication skills to do this, so they occupy a special place in our imaginations. They remind us that when we were very young we believed that we *could* communicate with other creatures, because there was no separation between their world and ours.

Dolphin intelligence comes in a different package than human intelligence, but a thread of awareness connects us. We recognize a kinship in one another, and this connection is something we seem to long for. In some deep way we hope to find other wisdom, other guidance—other companions in life. It's the reason we point telescopes toward the stars and wonder if there's anyone out there who wants to talk to us. Even the tiniest possibility that the answer might be yes both terrifies and thrills us. Given our curiosity about the meaning of our lives, and our place in the bigger scheme of things, it's pretty reasonable to wonder if behind their Mona Lisa smiles, dolphins might be in on some good cosmic secrets.

When I think back on it now, my swim with the spinners in Honolua Bay was an experience as mystifying as it was uplifting. Who *were* those creatures? It's been said that humans are the only animals who believe the stories they tell about themselves—but what about the dolphins? What is their story? And what about those haunting sounds they made? Their whistles and clicks and squeals seemed to me like a liquid symphony, a message from another galaxy, in a language that defied translation. When I saw the pod, I felt joy. I felt awe. And I felt the slightest bit frightened, though the dolphins were not scary. I felt their beguiling mystery. I felt a sense of bottomless wonder.

The one thing I didn't feel was alone.

Chapter 2

The Meaning of Water

≈≈≈

*A*bove anything else, I wanted to meet up with the dolphins again. The urge to get back into the ocean and look for them was so strong that, over the next year, I reshuffled all my priorities. I set my job aside. I put all the obligations in my life on hold. My goal was simple, if not easy: to travel the world exploring the strange and ancient relationship between humans and dolphins. My reasons? Because the idea of such a quest made me happy—and my father would have encouraged it. Because I was too curious *not* to follow wherever the dolphins might lead me. Because I wondered if there was some greater understanding possible at the place where our world and theirs intersected. And because I really wanted an answer to this one question: why had a mere ten minutes in the dolphins' presence been such a soul-shaking experience?

I knew where I wanted to go first: back to Hawaii. But this time, I headed to the Big Island. Though it is officially (and confusingly) called Hawaii, the Big Island got its nickname for a good reason: it's big. You could fit Maui, Oahu, Kauai, Lanai, and Kahoolawe inside it and still have plenty of room to spare. Born from five feisty volcanoes, the Big Island is also the state's youngest island. It's more than five hundred thousand years old, but in geological terms it's still a baby. Much of its terrain is stark black lava rock, not yet covered by plants, and its landscape is rugged. Steering my rental car out of the Kona airport I saw Mauna Loa, the world's largest active volcano, and another massive volcano, Mauna Kea.

If you followed Mauna Kea down to the seafloor, you'd be measuring a mountain higher than Mount Everest; most of the volcano lies underwater. At its peak I could make out the glinting domes of thirteen telescopes, famous perches from which astronomers study the night sky. Here in the middle of the Pacific Ocean, far from the lights of cities, they can more clearly glimpse the heavens than anywhere else on the planet—the billions of stars, the planets and their many moons, the solar systems with their nebulas and starbursts and voids, the asteroids and comets and supernovas, our sun and other suns, all the question marks floating out in space. "Hawaii is Earth's connecting point to the rest of the universe," the Mauna Kea Observatories' website proclaims.

But I had come to the Big Island to look down, rather than up. It was the universe below the ocean's surface that interested me: these waters teemed with dolphins. There were hundreds of spinners here, and each morning they appeared so reliably in certain bays along this coastline that a community of people had formed around them. They called it Dolphinville, though it was less an actual place than a shared state of mind. "There are approximately 200 of us, and we live in separate homes along a 30-mile stretch of the Kona coast, connected in spirit to each other," I read, in a description of the group. "Many of us who live here have been called by the dolphins. We have become like a family who swim, meditate, and work together. Swimming among the dolphins day after day, we are in deep communication with them." Above this description there was a group photo with dozens of suntanned, smiling people who seemed like they were having a lot more fun than anyone I knew back on the mainland. Nobody looked crazy.

I was intrigued to learn about Dolphinville, especially when I found out that the group's creator (or pod leader, maybe) was a woman named Joan Ocean. A New Jersey–

born psychologist turned New Age dolphin guru, Ocean had logged over twenty thousand hours with wild dolphins. When I'd emailed to see if I could come to the Big Island and join her for a swim, she'd responded yes, and also invited me to stay at her house.

Since the sixties, dolphin research had progressed fast, revealing much about the animals' behavior and bodies and brains, but the more we learned, it seemed, the more we needed to make sense of our findings, not only with our minds but also with our hearts. I knew the questions I was asking couldn't be answered just by reading scientific papers or marine mammal textbooks, fascinating as those were. My answers could only be found in the ocean.

~~~~~~

"I call what I do 'participatory research,'" Joan Ocean said, standing barefoot on the harbor dock, flashing a smile. We were waiting, along with about twenty other people, for a boat called *Sunlight on Water* to start up its engines and take us out in search of local dolphin pods. The morning was bright, the sea an inviting marine blue. While everyone else carried the usual dorky snorkeling gear, Ocean held a pair of free-diving fins with long, sleek blades. Among the crowd of tourists, she stood out. Her hair was a tangle of silver and blond, but it was her eyes you noticed first. They were a brilliant shade of aquamarine, with an excited, kidlike energy. She wore a flowing cover-up over a black bathing suit, and sparkly pink toenail polish. At seventy-four years old, Ocean was a great-grandmother, but she looked oddly ageless. "If you wanted to learn about any culture, you would move in with them if they allowed it, and observe them and then try to be like them," she continued. "So that's what happened with the dolphins. The first twelve years I lived here, every single morning I was in the water. You just learn a lot."

When Ocean first became fascinated with dolphins back in the early eighties, she didn't even know how to swim; she was forty-five when she took her first stroke. But she quickly made up for lost time, regularly swimming miles at a stretch. The new saltwater world she had discovered "was like being on another planet, only better." In the years before she became immersed in dolphins, Ocean had been a psychologist. She'd counseled delinquent teenagers, troubled adults, broken families. She tried to coax her clients out of destructive patterns, only to watch in frustration when they repeated themselves. She prayed and meditated, asking for better ways to help people. What she got back in her mind's eye were images of dolphins (and the occasional whale). She began to seek them out: bottlenoses in Florida, orcas in British Columbia, spinners in Hawaii, botos in Brazil. Every encounter with them lifted her spirits—why, she wondered, wouldn't this be the same for others? She felt the animals were communicating messages of love and wisdom, somehow providing information we desperately needed to know. From that point on, Ocean's purpose was clear: introducing people to cetaceans.

The resident Kona pods, she explained, lived in what was known as a "fission-fusion" society. Basically, the mass of dolphins moved in fluid, constantly changing groups, like people milling around at a party. This was a sophisticated arrangement, uncommon in nature, requiring the animals to recognize one another, form bonds, trade favors, recall past associations, and get along in unfamiliar circumstances. Scientists had wondered what made dolphins decide to leave one group or join another; they discovered that dolphins moved between social clusters for the same reasons humans might. A teenage dolphin swimming along with his mother, for instance, might defect to a band of teenage dolphins who were having fun; females with calves liked to hang out together; mating pairs were mostly interested in one another. In dangerous situations or tricky hunting conditions these groups would merge together into one larger pod. When the heat was off, they would drift apart again. To researchers, it seemed likely that the spinners along this coast all knew one another, at least on an acquaintance basis.

Ocean was quick to point out that she was not a scientist. "I didn't choose that particular path," she said. But she knew these dolphins. She had observed them in action, day in, day out, for twenty-six years. She knew their habits and their quirks, their likes and dislikes and the body language that expressed them, their fondness for playing with the gold-colored leaves that fluttered from hala trees into the ocean. She recognized individuals and charted the company each dolphin kept; she noticed when one animal showed up with a cookiecutter shark bite, or another bore signs of a boat propeller strike. She knew their rhythms. Each morning after dawn, pretty much like clockwork, the spinners would return from a night of feeding in deeper waters and move into the island's shallower bays, circling slowly, schmoozing with one another, and in general taking it easy until midafternoon, when they'd begin to head offshore again. This nocturnal hunting schedule was for good reason: at night, schools of fish, squid, and shrimp rose from the depths and became a dolphin's all-you-can-eat buffet.

It would be hard to find someone more excited about dolphins than Ocean, I thought. Her life choices added up to the opposite of a normal career. Imagine writing this on a job description: "swimming with dolphins in the ocean as much as possible." It seems highly unlikely that you could make a living at that. But Ocean had managed it. These days, dolphin lovers from all over the world flew to Hawaii to attend her weeklong workshops, which were often sold out months in advance.

Sunlight on Water floated quietly in its slip while its passengers fumbled with flippers, cameras, sunblock. After a Hawaiian prayer of thanks to *kala,* the sun, we set off. The crew consisted of the captain, Jason, assisted by first mate, Dusty. Jason and Dusty were suntanned young guys who looked like they would rather be surfing than baby-sitting a boatload of tourists. As we chugged out of the harbor, Ocean listened politely as Dusty gave advice about swimming with wild dolphins: "So yeah, try to be mellow. The more mellow you are, the more calm and wise you're putting out there, the more they're gonna be into you. That Olympic champion Michael Phelps kind of swimming? You don't want to do that around the dolphins. They think that is aggressive behavior. It will make them not want to hang out with you. They're very awesome."

"How long do they live?" a stout woman asked in a Texas drawl.

"Uh, twenty, maybe twenty-five years—"

"Well, that's in captivity," Ocean cut in. "We don't

really know how long they live, but I have all the notes from the first researcher here, Ken Norris, years and years ago. The dolphins he was studying are still here, a lot of them. So we have some pretty good evidence that they live longer than people think. And whales can live to be a hundred."

Ocean and I sat together at the stern, watching the water. The Kona coast slid by in the clear morning light, spray from the boat's wake casting tiny diamonds into the sky. It was an ideal day to meet up with the spinners—and I knew they would be here. We were headed into the center of their universe, the best place to go if you wanted to find them.

The large number of dolphins who lived near this island was a big draw for scientists. Along with the spinners, they could also find more exotic dolphin species here, deep-water creatures like pilot whales, false killer whales, rough-toothed dolphins, striped dolphins, dwarf killer whales, Risso's dolphins, and melon-headed whales. Bottlenose and spotted dolphins regularly showed up, too.

The man whose name Ocean had mentioned, Ken Norris, was a famous dolphin scientist. He had studied Hawaii's spinner population from the 1960s through the 1980s. During that time, he discovered many surprising facts about dolphins, describing them as the most mysterious animals on the planet. Norris proved that dolphins were masters of the world of sound, and he was able to show how they used their sonar to create pictures of their surroundings, down to the subtlest detail. Even blindfolded, for instance, a dolphin could tell the difference between a piece of copper and a piece of aluminum. The dolphins' amazing abilities fascinated Norris, and he wondered why the animals had developed them. It's not like they needed to be aquatic Einsteins in order to hang out with sea turtles and jellyfish. What, exactly, were they using their impressive brains for? He'd had a glimpse of what the dolphins could do—the next step was to figure out why they were doing it.

Norris's research began just five miles south of here, in Kealake'akua Bay, a dramatic inlet ringed by sea cliffs. (Translated from Hawaiian, its name means "Pathway of the Gods.") Along with its abundant dolphins, Kealake'akua was known for its memorable snorkeling, storybook sunsets, and notorious history: it was the place where Captain James Cook landed in 1779 and then, in a fight with natives over the theft of a boat, was stabbed to death.

"The Kealake'akua Bay topography was perfect for dolphin work," Norris wrote. "A magnificent, nearly vertical five-hundred-foot cliff loomed over the almost-always calm and clear semicircular bay. A group of dolphins rested in the bay nearly every day. One could look down almost on top of those resting dolphins, and their behavior could often be seen . . . as they moved offshore, until they faded from view into the gray disk of the sea."

Ocean, too, wanted to watch the dolphins up close, and while the scientists went about their work, she continued to swim in her backyard—Kealake'akua Bay. From the small house she rented on its rocky shores, she would venture out to meet the spinners. She swam with them on cloudy choppy days and stormy rainy days and flat overcast days and days when the sun blasted down. She swam with them every single day for twelve years. At times, other people joined her, but much of the time, even far offshore, Ocean swam alone.

"I've always been guided by the dolphins," she told me. "I could totally trust them—they would never crash me into coral or take me out to sea. I could swim eye to eye with them for hours. I never had to look up, I could breathe through my snorkel." Swimming like this for extended periods, Ocean said, made her mind slow down and her worries slip away. "As time went on and I became completely at home in the water," she said, "I began to understand their language."

The boat slowed as Jason drove into Kailua Bay, a

curved shoreline dotted with hotels, stores, and restaurants. The water was calm here, making it a favorite spot for swimmers, paddleboarders, and kayakers. Several other dolphin-watching boats idled in the bay. Once my eyes adjusted to the sunlight's glare, I realized there were hundreds of dolphins in here.

Jason cut the engines. "Pool's open!" he yelled, and with that, Ocean and I slid into the water. Immediately, she swam off in the direction of the pods. I followed. The water was warm, and I could see all the way to the seafloor, sixty feet down and speckled with reefs. Fish cruised near the bottom. I was startled by the contrast between the peacefulness below the surface and the activity above as people clambered off and onto boats. But the dolphins were nowhere in sight.

I knew from my reading that spinners are shy by nature, and prefer to be the ones to initiate a meeting. When you dump a bunch of snorkelers near them they tend to back off, regroup, and then decide how much contact they want. Unlike bottlenose dolphins, who often want to play with humans, the spinners are reserved, almost standoffish. "I always tell people, don't swim after them," Ocean had warned. "You'll just wear yourself out. They'll circle outside of all the boats and all the people. They don't go away— they're circling. But in the beginning when everyone gets into the water, it's like mayhem. The dolphins will sonar the people and wait for them to calm down."

Adjusting my mask, I scanned the other snorkelers I could see in the bay. About twenty feet away, a guy in neon-green surf trunks swam by holding a GoPro camera mounted on a long pole, his legs pumping, churning away in his fins. His head snapped back and forth, surveying the ocean impatiently. His aggressive body language annoyed me; I suspected the dolphins felt the same.

Then, far below, I saw them. A dozen spinners glided by, fin to fin. They were thirty feet down and all I could do was admire their hazy outlines from above, but it was enough to captivate me. These dolphins were part of a larger group, and when the rest of the pod flowed past, every person in the vicinity shot off after them. Even the most sluggish dolphin was moving far faster than flailing snorkelers could match, however, so this was a bad strategy. "They're better swimmers than we are," Dusty had pointed out. "If you chase them, all you'll see today is a bit of receding tail."

Ocean took off in the opposite direction, and I followed her as she dove to twenty feet, kicking strongly. Almost instantly, three dolphins appeared in front of her. Ocean dove deeper, tucking in behind them. The dolphins arched to the surface, breaking through to breathe before diving again. Somehow each dolphin knew precisely what the other dolphins were about to do, and they moved effortlessly as one.

We spent the morning in Kailua Bay because the dolphins stayed there, too, orbiting us. Every so often they'd cut through the bay, allowing us a few moments in their company. The encounters were brief; Ocean referred to them as drive-bys. Still, it was fascinating to watch such a sprawling pod of dolphins, even if they weren't that interested in us.

At one point a manta ray cruised by, its great black kite of a body rippling over the seafloor, its whip of a tail trailing elegantly behind. I stared at it for so long that I almost missed the two dolphins who were hovering behind me, looking at me with interest. These were not spinners, I could tell immediately. They were bigger, thicker, and not shy at all. One of them moved closer and swung his head toward me, and I felt him zap me with a burst of sonar. Then I heard him make some creaking noises, like a door swinging back and forth on rusty hinges. Our eyes met, and he nodded his head repeatedly. It felt as though we were having a heated conversation, but I had no idea what it was about.

Having sized me up, the alpha dolphins swam past me to a man on a paddleboard nearby. I didn't usually think of dolphins as intimidating creatures, but these two reminded me of that possibility. Earlier, Ocean had told me how she'd once been whacked so hard on the leg by a dolphin's tail that she couldn't walk afterward; on another occasion a bottlenose had clamped his jaws on her calf, staring at her and refusing to let go. "People think, 'Oh, dolphins, all sugary sweet and loving,'" Ocean said, with a laugh. "And they are—but they also have such power."

As the morning continued, the bay gradually emptied of snorkelers and the spinners seemed to relax, swimming slower and coming closer. This was their version of sleep, after all—and who can doze in the middle of Grand Central Station? Dolphins never actually shut both eyes and nod off like we do. Unlike us, they are conscious breathers. Whenever dolphins take in oxygen it's a decision, not an automatic body function, which makes sense if you think about it: they are air-breathing mammals who live underwater. If a dolphin were knocked out and his body continued to try to take in air, he would drown. Dolphins themselves seem to understand this: when a dolphin loses consciousness his podmates will lift him to the surface, holding him up there until he's revived.

Because each breath is intentional, dolphins have to keep swimming, stay awake, maintain system operations at all times. Physically, this is a tall order. Imagine if instead of snoozing under a fluffy duvet, you had to bicycle an easy hundred miles in your sleep. This would destroy us, but dolphins are able to do it because they operate the two hemispheres of their brain independently. While one side runs the show, the other side rests. It's an impressive juggling act: even when they nap, dolphins are always at least half-awake.

After a while I became cold and returned to the boat. Most of the other passengers were already on deck, eating pineapple slices and comparing dolphin stories. A ten-year-old girl told her mother excitedly, over and over: "They swam right next to me! They swam right next to me!"

Suddenly, off the bow, a spinner shot out of the water, leaping into the air and whirling at least five times. Another dolphin followed seconds later, doing a full aerial somersault. Everyone cheered and clapped. "That right there was a blessing!" the woman from Texas yelled. Ocean smiled, towel drying her hair. "Why do they spin?" I asked. "Is it about mating or—"

"Fun," Ocean said. "It's more like fun. They seem to do a lot of things for fun." But it also had to do with signaling to one another, she added, and removing remoras, the suckerfish that attach themselves to the dolphins' skin and then hitchhike along feeding on bits of fish, or plankton, or anything else that comes their way. "I had a remora on my leg once," Ocean told me, with a smile. "It was the cutest little thing. But it hurt!"

"Do you ever feel as though you could just stay down there?" I asked. "Find a pod and just keep going?" Ocean laughed, and nodded: "All the time."

Chapter 3

Clappy, Clappy!

~~~~~~~~~

*T*he next stop on my dolphin journey was the Dominican Republic, a bright and lively Caribbean country
about twice the size of New Hampshire. I flew there to
visit Ocean World Adventure Park, a marine park that advertised itself as "the largest man-made dolphin habitat in
the world." Instead of meeting dolphins in their own environment, the idea here was that the dolphins were plucked
from the ocean and installed in a series of pools. People
could pay to swim with the captives.

I stood in the ticket line, looking at posters of people
posing with the creatures that lived inside these gates, including sixteen dolphins, a family of sea lions, a cage full
of parrots, and a pair of tigers in a fake stone grotto, caged
behind a thick sheet of plastic.

Ocean World is a place that encourages touching. At other marine parks, people must sit in the bleachers and watch dolphins doing choreographed tricks; here, they could pay to become part of the show. Visitors might ride a dolphin by latching onto its dorsal fin or be kissed on the mouth by a dolphin or have a dolphin pretend to dance with them. They might be licked on the head by a sea lion, or pet a stingray with its stinger removed, or stroke a nurse shark's sandpapery skin.

On the day I stopped by, it was the height of winter and I expected to see flocks of sunshine-seeking tourists streaming through Ocean World's gates, but the place was not crowded. I walked in and paused for a moment to get my bearings: Ocean World sprawls over thirty acres. The last time I had visited a marine park was in the late 1960s, in Fort Lauderdale, Florida, when I was four or five years old. Coincidentally, its name had also been Ocean World. In my hazy childhood memory it was an exotic place, filled with creatures I'd never imagined, like flamingos, alligators, and hammerhead sharks.

There were dolphins there, too, and when they weren't performing their dolphin show you could feed them, dropping little fish into their mouths. Though it was an outdated place, Ocean World Fort Lauderdale kept its doors open until 1994. It finally closed after being charged with animal abuse by the US Department of Agriculture. Among other violations, it was cited for cramming its dolphins into tiny, overchlorinated pools, inadequate veterinary care, dumping sewage into a nearby river, and "the improper burial of dolphins in the park's landscaping."

Now, decades later, I had come to this (unrelated) Ocean World to find out what life was like for the dolphins who lived there, because it is impossible to talk about dolphins without considering this fact: people will pay a lot of money to be with them. What other animal could entice a family of four to drop $800 in one afternoon? It was only the dolphins who commanded these fees.

The weather in the Dominican Republic was searingly hot, and the unshaded walkways and dolphin pools baked in the tropical glare. I stopped by the sea lion tank and took a long drink from my water bottle. Much concrete had been poured here, contributing to the fiendish temperatures. Beneath the peppy samba music, Ocean World felt vaguely threatening, with armed security guards posted around the property. NO GUNS OR WEAPONS ALLOWED WITHIN OCEAN WORLD PREMISES, warned a sign on the side of a building.

The park's dolphins were housed in a man-made lagoon divided by pathways and docks. There were one or two dolphins in each pen; below the docks, wire netting separated the enclosures. Most of the dolphins hung at the surface, barely moving. One of the dolphins trailed along-side me, staring up at me while I walked. Another nudged half-heartedly at a floating red ball.

Every dolphin here was a bottlenose, which was not surprising. Marine parks rely on this species because they usually fare better in captivity than other types of dolphins and learn quickly to perform tricks. (Orcas and beluga whales are popular attractions, too, though their size makes them more difficult to keep; when removed from the wild, both species tend to die at alarming rates.) Marine parks have also exhibited less familiar species like Amazon river dolphins, Risso's dolphins, pilot whales, white-sided dolphins, melon-headed whales, spinner dolphins, Fra-ser's dolphins, Commerson's dolphins, pantropical spotted dolphins, striped dolphins, common dolphins, and false killer whales—but none of them lasted too long. History has shown that dolphins of every species, bottlenose in-cluded, have a hard time living in tanks, and though some individuals adapt better than others, many captive dol-phins fall short—and often far short—of their natural life expectancies.

I knew this fact and I found it upsetting. I'm not a big fan of canned tourist experiences, especially when they are obviously all about making money, as this one seemed to be. As a rule, I don't enjoy watching tigers caged behind a casino, or dolphins recruited to tow people around a fake lagoon. At the same time, I wanted to find out what was going on in these tanks, if there was any possible benefit for humans or dolphins in this arrangement. I am a fan of top-notch facilities like the Monterey Bay Aquarium in Northern California, where every exhibit is rooted in the latest marine science and where admission profits go directly into important ocean research—but trained dolphins are not part of their plan. Dolphin shows and dolphin petting zoos are another business entirely, probably because each new finding about dolphins reveals them to be even more self-aware and socially advanced than we previously realized, and this raises hard questions about the morality of keeping such sophisticated creatures penned up, making them do our bidding in order to eat. Real dolphin science does not coexist easily with a place like Ocean World.

But people don't always think about the details, and they come to marine parks like this one and plan family vacations around dolphin captivity—and I would imagine that most of these people have good intentions and would insist that they absolutely love dolphins, even as the animals orbit their tiny pools as endlessly as lost satellites. Relentless advertising pushes the image of dolphins as happy ambassadors to all humanity. The marine parks insist that they are providing a vital educational service, one that aids dolphins and builds awareness of the ocean and helps ensure the conservation of the animals that live there. All of which are worthy endeavors, of course, and I was prepared to upgrade my impressions if any of these claims were true.

I had chosen the thirty-minute dolphin swim, so I changed into my bathing suit and followed the signs to a thatch-roofed snack bar called the Dolphin Hut. There, I was given a yellow life jacket and herded in with a group of seven other people. We bunched together in a patch of shade while an Ocean World employee laid out the rules, holding up a stuffed dolphin to demonstrate. "Do not hit them or smack them," he said. "They don't like that. And don't touch them in the blowhole. That is their private area."

Orientation over, we were directed down the dock to a semicircular enclosure, where two trainers awaited. The water in this pool was darker blue and intended to look like an actual pond or a miniature lake, with little visibility below. One of the trainers stepped onto a floating platform and set down a plastic cooler. The moment he did this, two bottlenose heads popped up in front of him. They had the excited, expectant vibe of puppies, except they were twelve-foot long, thousand-pound wild animals, which became clear when I saw them up close. These dolphins made the spinners in Hawaii look like bath toys.

We sat in a row along the side of the platform, our legs dangling in the water. The dolphins dove, shot around the tank, and then reappeared in front of the cooler. The second trainer, a guy I'll call Alonso, began by introducing them. "This is Serena and Niagara," he said, pointing to the dolphins. They had their heads out of the water and their mouths open and I could see their thick pink tongues, lined by perfectly spaced teeth that looked like sharpened pine nuts. Both dolphins had silvery bodies and the softest, palest pink tinge on their underbellies. "They like being together," Alonso told us, adding: "If they don't get along, they fight." He made punching motions with his fists. The dolphins stared hungrily. Opening the cooler, Alonso flicked two tiny fish at Serena and Niagara. "Clappy, clappy!" he yelled, waving his hands. The dolphins rose out of the water vertically and beat their fins on the surface, soaking the people, who screamed in delight.

During our thirty-minute swim the dolphins performed a series of tricks, none of which seemed to engage them even slightly, and all of which seemed, if you stopped for half a second to think about it, depressingly dumb. Serena and Niagara leaped over our heads, and dragged us around the tank, and pressed their beaks to our faces on command. Whenever they completed a trick, they raced over to the cooler and resumed their begging posture.

In the end, not even the concrete gloom of Ocean

World could squelch the magic of Serena and Niagara, who seemed in all ways more interesting than their trainers, and who were obviously capable of feats on a completely different scale. But Ocean World's program did not involve teaching anyone anything about the incredible real lives of wild dolphins. Not even the slightest ocean conservation message was offered.

As Serena and Niagara completed their routine, I was struck by the dull look in their eyes and the intensity of their focus on the fish, as though they had been waiting for that cooler to appear for a very long time. While I was thinking about this, I heard Alonso ask the group: "Do you know how long these dolphins live?"

"Twenty years?" a teenage girl answered, guessing wrongly. (Bottlenose dolphins can easily live at least twice that long.)

"Yes!" Alonso said, grinning and revealing a set of mismatched teeth. "But only in here. In the ocean, they live shorter." He held up a cautionary index finger. "In the ocean their life is very hard."

~~~~~~

It was P. T. Barnum, the circus showman, who first exhibited cetaceans back in 1861. Once he discovered that vast beluga whale pods congregated in northeastern Canada, he collected two of the animals and shipped them to his American Museum in New York. With their Casper the Friendly Ghost appearance, their impressive size, and their sweet dispositions, the belugas were a huge draw in the hours they survived. They shared the second floor of the museum with a stuffed elephant, an electric eel, an alligator, a seal who played the harmonica, a fat lady, a one-armed, one-legged soldier, and a giantess named Miss Swan, who sat on an oversize throne.

"In August last I succeeded in bringing to the Museum two living white whales from Labrador," Barnum wrote. "One died the first day and the other the second day. Even in this brief period, thousands availed themselves of the opportunity of witnessing this rare sight. Since August I have brought two more whales to New York, at enormous expense, but both died before I could get them into the Museum." Once again, Barnum returned to Canada to snatch up more belugas. At least nine belugas rotated through Barnum's exhibit, all of whom died promptly. Then, in 1865, the museum burned to the ground, taking another two belugas with it. In an article about the fire, the *New York Times* mourned the loss of the whales and their "fearful death by roasting."

Bottlenose dolphins leaped onto the scene in 1938,

with the opening of Marine Studios, in St. Augustine, Florida. Billed as the world's first "oceanarium," Marine Studios was originally built as an underwater movie set, stocked with sea creatures who could be filmed through portholes in two enormous steel tanks. It was a grand project, and an expensive one. Someone came up with the idea of selling tickets to the public to offset operating costs.

From the start, the place was a hit. On opening day, thirty thousand people showed up to peer through the portholes at the gleaming coral reef, the schools of jewel-colored fish, the sea turtles and moray eels and stingrays and tiger sharks gliding by. In 1938, America was limping out of the Great Depression, scuba had not been invented yet, and no one had seen this underwater world before. A helmeted diver walked the tank floor feeding the barracudas and goliath groupers by hand. Sun-dappled sea horses tipped in the current; moon-colored octopi jetted under rocks. It must have been hypnotic and wonderful, like a submarine dream of the ocean, now available on land.

Marine Studios' most popular feature was its dolphins, one of whom swam around carrying a sign in his mouth that said I AM A BOTTLENOSED DOLPHIN. This wasn't the bottlenoses' first public appearance—the New York Aquarium had some as early as 1913—but it was here that dolphins were first trained to do tricks. To everyone's excitement new animals were constantly added to the tanks, including more bottlenoses, spotted dolphins, and even the occasional pilot whale.

Dolphins came and went during the fifties, plucked from the nearby Atlantic Ocean by Marine Studios' forty-eight-foot collecting boat, *The Porpoise*. Pretty quickly, it became clear that some dolphins were smarter and easier to manage than others. Eventually, a star emerged: a male bottlenose named Flippy. Advertised as "the World's Most Educated Dolphin," Flippy could shoot basketballs and throw footballs and push a dog around on a surfboard. He could fly through hoops. In 1955, he starred in the sequel to the movie *Creature from the Black Lagoon*.

Flippy was soon eclipsed by Flipper, a charismatic bottlenose dolphin who ended up starring in a movie and his own television show. Though Flipper was a male character, on TV he was played by a rotating cast of five female dolphins. Each week, Flipper rescued his adopted human family from dangers that included underwater explosions and shark attacks. The show was a big hit—everyone loved Flipper.

Flipper's popularity spread quickly from Florida, where the show was filmed, to the rest of North America, splashing into even the most landlocked places. Suddenly, everybody wanted to see dolphins in action. In the dolphin-mania that followed—which has only grown since Flipper's time—marine parks have become a multibillion-dollar global industry. Swim-with-dolphins programs are now being launched at the rate of two per year throughout the Caribbean, and can now be found even in far-flung places like Romania and Cambodia.

~~~~~~~

When our thirty minutes were over the enclosure emptied of people, and the trainers packed up their cooler and wandered off, too. I stood on the walkway watching Serena and Niagara circling, visibly aware that the fish were gone. Music pounded through speakers, so loud it made the railings vibrate. I wondered what it was like for the dolphins to be subjected to so much noise all day. Sound is a physical force; when we're bombarded by it we come apart quickly (imagine being locked in a room with someone running a jackhammer or screaming at the top of their lungs). Excessive noise bugs us and hurts us. It damages our nervous systems, circulation, mental health, and of course, our ears. Dolphins, with their ability to hear across far wider frequencies, are especially vulnerable. After a thirty-six-hour dance party was held near their enclosure at Conny-Land, a Swiss marine park, two dolphins died the next day.

Conny-Land had often been criticized for how it treated its dolphins. In the park's twenty-five-year history the animals had died from many causes, including infections, sunburn, freezing, heat stroke, brain damage, chlorine burns, heart attacks, poisoning, jumping out of their tanks, and mushrooms getting stuck in their intestines.

It's unclear how a dolphin ends up jammed full of mushrooms, but dolphins are curious animals, and they will often pick up and swallow things that get dropped in their tanks. Scientists have puzzled over why this happens so much in captivity, why dolphins with their fine-tuned sonar might suddenly mistake a leather glove or a french fry container for food. They suspect that when marine parks train dolphins to eat dead fish—in the ocean, of course, they hunt live prey—the animals become confused and start nibbling at anything they encounter. This is a dangerous practice for dolphins. It causes intestinal blockages, which are usually fatal. Pieces of plastic are a common killer, but dolphins have also died from eating bottle caps, coins, car keys, coffee cups, roofing tiles, cigarette lighters, balloons, rubber toys, jewelry, steel wool, nails, and chunks of cement.

The other likely culprit is boredom. If your entire world were a swimming pool, you would probably take great interest in examining the stuff people tossed in, too. For a creature as smart and creative and sociable as a dolphin, life in a blank white concrete tank is a cruel fate. Biologist Toni Frohoff, who studies stress in captive dolphins, has watched the animals chew on their cement enclosures until their teeth are ground down, and bang themselves repeatedly against the walls. Stressed-out dolphins, like stressed-out people, develop ulcers, have heart attacks, and suffer from weakened immune systems. They succumb easily to infections like pneumonia, hepatitis, and meningitis.

Some dolphins learn to tolerate captivity, but even the biggest enclosures can never match the vast ocean, where the animals travel for miles in close-knit groups, hunting and playing in ever-changing conditions. Out there, in the depths and the shallows, they work as a team, devising clever fish-catching strategies on the fly. In Shark Bay, Australia, one group of bottlenoses uses sea sponges like protective gloves, covering the tips of their beaks with them when they forage in the rough sand on the seafloor, digging for burrowing fish. In other locations, dolphins blow bubble curtains or stir up mud plumes to trap schools of fish. Orcas have been filmed lining up in a row and using their tails to generate waves that flush seals off an ice floe. In every environment, the dolphins will figure out a plan. In heavy surf, in calm bays, in clear tropical seas and murky rivers, in kelp forests and eelgrass channels, in moonlight and sunlight and the darkest depths of the ocean, they go about their business together.

Only now are we beginning to understand what that word, *together*, means to a dolphin. In the wild, dolphins are minglers, gadabouts, flirts. Their existence revolves around relationships. Like us, dolphins form intense, long-term attachments with others, and they maintain them over time, even when they're separated for long periods. Scientist Jason Bruck, from the University of Chicago, proved that dolphins recognize their friends' signature whistles even after twenty years apart, and react with excitement when they hear them. Their bonds are so strong, in fact, that when dolphins are in danger they will not leave one another even if it costs them their lives. And when dolphins do lose a loved one, they behave in ways that suggest they are feeling deep grief.

Often, marine parks claim that dolphins are happier in cement tanks because it saves them the trouble of finding their own fish in our increasingly ruined oceans. But even if the dolphins are being served tuna sashimi on a silver tray in luxury hotel suites, the truth remains that in captivity their lives are hollowed out. In a concrete tank none of their skills are needed, not their sonar or their hunting skills or their amazing communication abilities. The friendships that sustain them are no longer part of their world. They become prisoners.

No wonder dolphins get sick, depressed, and anxious. No wonder marine parks mix antibiotics and antianxiety medications into their food. Just like people, dolphins express their emotions in personal ways. Some dolphins mope and despair. Others vent their feelings through aggression—they fight. Tooth raking, jaw clapping, tail lashing, head butting, biting, and high-speed chasing are common behaviors among upset dolphins; animals have died from skull fractures after leaping out of their tanks to escape the beatings. At SeaWorld San Diego, Kandu, a five-thousand-pound female orca from Iceland, slammed into Corky, a seven-thousand-pound female orca from Canada, fracturing her own jaw and rupturing an artery in the process, causing blood to spurt through her blowhole. While thousands of people looked on from their seats, and the water in the tank turned bright red, Kandu bled to death. SeaWorld described the incident as a "normal, socially induced act of aggression." Scientists from the Humane Society disagreed. They pointed out that in the wild, orcas from different oceans would not end up crammed together in a small space, and that normally orcas didn't behave this way.

Sometimes people get hurt, too. At SeaWorld Orlando's Dolphin Cove, a bottlenose chomped down on a seven-year-old boy's hand and held on, even as two people tried to pry his jaws apart. One man had his sternum cracked during a dolphin encounter; another woman had her ribs broken. Some swim-with-dolphins clientele have had their teeth knocked out. In one recent episode, a bottlenose jumped out of the water above a group of tourists, and then landed on them purposely.

An angry bottlenose can do some serious damage, but the dangers grow with the animals' size: orcas, the largest species of dolphin, have their own terrifying record. "Any person who has trained these animals has been thumped, bumped, bruised, bitten and otherwise abused over the course of time," one trainer told the *San Diego Union* newspaper. A widely used training handbook listed some aggressive behaviors of orcas as "butting, biting, grabbing, dunking and holding trainers on the bottom of pools and preventing their escape." While orcas have never fatally attacked humans anywhere in the world's oceans, in captivity orcas have injured their trainers hundreds of times. And tragically, on four occasions people have been killed by orcas at marine parks.

I stayed for a while longer watching Serena and Niagara circling, alone in their pool. The sun was setting and the afternoon light ripened to apricot gold and the water took on a metallic sheen as the reflections melted into shadow. Over by the lagoon, I saw trainers walking briskly down the docks to feed the dolphins who hadn't performed in shows. The men all carried the same thrilling plastic cooler, and the dolphins leaped in their pens when they saw it. One dolphin rose out of the water and began to tail-walk, as if auditioning for fish. In a bathtub-size enclosure, set off to the side, two Ocean World employees knelt next to a bottlenose who was floating quietly. A clear plastic tube ran from the dolphin's blowhole into a metal canister that was in turn plugged into an electrical socket, as though the animal were being vacuumed out. When one of the men turned and saw me looking at them, he signaled at me angrily to get lost.

I was startled by this unfriendly gesture, and moved so I was behind a sign and out of his line of sight. Serena swam over to me, stopping in front of the railing where I stood. She lifted her head from the water and then rolled onto her side, as if trying to examine me from several angles. Unlike the mellow little spinners, these bottlenose dolphins seemed to be actively trying to reach across the divide between their species and ours. I could see why the scientists who worked closely with them were moved by the experience.

As I turned to leave, Alonso walked by. I nodded at him and started toward the exit, but then I remembered a question I had wanted to ask: "Hey," I called, getting his attention. "Where do these dolphins come from?" He stopped, and looked at me for a long moment. "Ah, that's a good question," he said. He was smiling, but his voice had an edge and his eyes were as hard as marbles. "We have one from Honduras, one from Cuba, and one from right over there." He waved vaguely toward the ocean. This did not add up to sixteen dolphins, obviously, but I didn't want to push it. I had asked a simple question but though I didn't know it at the time, a highly sensitive one. Alonso's answer was a clumsy attempt to avoid it. What I also didn't know was that months later, when I learned the real stories of how dolphins are captured from the wild, they would pull me like an undertow, deep below the surface, into a world of darkness.

Chapter 4

The Friendlies

*O*n Ireland's Dingle Peninsula, there are many places with strange names, like Lios Póil and Ballyferriter and Foilatrisnig. There is Tralee, a town with sod-roofed houses that look like they were built by hobbits, and Ballnavenooragh, with its elaborate stone fort, and Riasc, the site of beehive-shaped huts that are 1,400 years old. The peninsula has medieval castles, Bronze Age tools and Iron Age weapons, and there are mysterious rocks lying around everywhere, carved with ancient symbols. Every village has its own haunting story. Every person who lives here has a strong, proud sense of his past. Then there's the town of Dingle itself, which has Fungie the Dingle Dolphin.

I had heard rumors about Fungie, a male bottlenose

who had left the open sea and decided instead to live inside Dingle's harbor, a shallow inlet bordered by low hills that are speckled with sheep. According to local legend, he had been swimming around in this small area since October 1983. It did not seem like the best place for a dolphin to settle. Though Dingle is sheltered from stormy North Atlantic conditions—churning seas, huffing winds—dolphins are well equipped for these things and seem to love the action: surfing down the faces of waves, leaping through the wakes of ships, playing in the tumult. By comparison, the Dingle harbor is a pond. After the dolphin, the next wildest animals in Dingle are cows.

Living inside the harbor would also expose Fungie to busy boat traffic, including the town's fleet of fishing trawlers, and the bay's quiet appearance hid the fact of its extreme tides. On some days the water's depth fluctuated as much as fifteen feet, a draining so drastic that if he wasn't careful a dolphin might easily end up beached in the mud. Dingle harbor couldn't be mistaken for a marine sanctuary, either: in the past it had been known for its abundant floating trash. So what was a full-grown bottlenose with an entire ocean available to him doing in this fish tank? And where was his pod? Whenever Fungie was spotted—almost every day, apparently—he was always alone.

Fungie has his own Facebook page and Twitter feed,

but I still wasn't sure if he really existed, so I decided to go to Ireland and see him for myself. Somehow, the stories I'd read about Fungie made him seem less like a real dolphin and more like a Disney character the town had invented to drum up tourism. It was hard to believe that the same adult bottlenose had lived in Dingle for the past thirty years. That would make him at least forty-two or forty-three years old, and though dolphins can certainly live to that age, Fungie's living situation was so unusual that it seemed like a long shot. Being part of a pod means protection, hunting success, society, kin—the basics of dolphin existence. So how did this solitary dolphin survive?

Dolphins are among the most social animals, so the idea of a loner bottlenose seemed unlikely. But surprisingly, Fungie is not the only one of his kind. In fact, I learned, there are many tales of dolphins who break away from their pods for reasons unknown—or are cast out or lost or orphaned—and end up seeking human companionship instead. These animals are usually bottlenoses, but there have also been instances of solitary orcas, spotted dolphins, common dolphins, dusky dolphins, Risso's dolphins, beluga whales, and even the rare tucuxi—a pink-bellied South American dolphin species—who decide to live in a small area and community of people, all by themselves.

Scientists don't know why it happens, but tales of dolphins befriending humans go far back into history. Many human-dolphin stories have similar themes: dolphins seek us out, dolphins want to play with us, dolphins try to help us, dolphins rescue us. If dolphins didn't already have such a well-established reputation for showing up like Superman, zooming in to help people who are in trouble in the ocean, their behavior would seem impossible to believe. But there are centuries and even millennia of tales of their generosity and kindness toward us. Dolphins have been known to respond like highly skilled lifeguards, saving people from all kinds of aquatic dangers. Occasionally they perform small kindnesses like retrieving lost diving gear or helping fishermen catch fish. It's hard to imagine that dolphins actually care about us—*us* being the ones who catch them in nets and poison them with chemicals and make them do silly tricks and, in certain parts of the world, eat them—but at least some of them act like they do.

The most amazing story I heard came from Maddalena Bearzi, a biologist who studies dolphins in Southern California. Bearzi recalls following a pod of bottlenoses on one foggy gray morning along the coast of Los Angeles. The dolphins were hunting, ignoring her research boat as they searched for fish. Finally, they found a big school of sardines and began herding them. If there's anything that gets a dolphin's attention, it's a big batch of fish, so Bearzi was surprised when one of the dolphins suddenly broke away and headed out to sea, swimming at top speed. The rest of the pod followed; so did Bearzi and her crew. The dolphins swam about three miles and then they stopped, and arranged themselves in a circle. In the center, the scientists were shocked to see a girl's body floating. She was a teenager and barely alive. Around her neck, the girl had wrapped a plastic bag containing her identification and a suicide note. Thanks to the dolphins, she was rescued.

Tales like this are remarkably common. Famously, when rescuers pulled five-year-old Cuban refugee Elián González out of the water three miles off Florida's coast, adrift and alone for forty-eight hours after his boat capsized and everyone else aboard had drowned, some of his first words were about how dolphins had surrounded him and kept him from slipping off his life preserver in stormy seas. I also heard several stories about dolphins protecting people from aggressive sharks. When surfer Todd Endris was bitten by a great white shark near Monterey, California, dolphins drove off the shark, formed a ring around Endris, and escorted him to the beach.

What should we think about these stories? One point

worth noting is that dolphins often behave toward us in the same ways they do toward one another. It is typical dolphin behavior to fend off sharks, or hold an injured mate at the surface so he can breathe, or steer the pod away from danger. In the dolphins' nomadic undersea world to be alone is to be vulnerable, so a single human in the water must seem to them greatly in need of help. Their consideration of us isn't limited to emergency situations, either: at the Tangalooma Island Resort in Australia, where wild bottlenoses are regularly fed fish by people standing in the shallows, biologists have documented—on twenty-three occasions—the dolphins offering gifts back to the people, swimming up to offer freshly caught tuna, eels, and octopi.

In other words, dolphins often act as though there's no difference between us and them. At times they don't seem to care that we are not members of their species—they simply appoint us honorary dolphins. Maybe that was why Fungie had made his home among the residents of Dingle. To him, perhaps, they were just a funny-looking pod.

〜〜〜〜

I drove down to Dingle from Dublin, winding through green and peaceful country, through bustling little cities and quaint little towns. The drive was pretty, but it was six hours long, and when I crested a final set of hills and dropped into the last valley before Dingle, I felt relief. In the distance, I could see a silvery bay that changed color to bruised lavender as clouds swept by overhead.

Dingle is a harbor town, and everything in it points toward the water. Its main street runs alongside the bay itself, a colorful row of stores, restaurants, and inns. Fishing boats float at the docks, two and three abreast, loaded with buoys and ropes and piles of netting. I parked my car and got out to take a look around. I knew I'd arrived at the right spot because in front of the harbor stood a life-size statue of Fungie, cast in gleaming bronze. Two kids sat on the dolphin's back eating croissants while their parents snapped pictures with their phones; other families stood nearby, waiting for their own photo opportunities. A small girl in a pink tracksuit ran around the statue shouting, "Fungie! Fungie! Fungie!"

I stood there for a moment watching; then I turned to a man holding a stroller next to me and asked if he had seen Fungie in person. The man looked surprised. "Oh, yes. I've seen him many times," he said, pointing to the water. He's always here." The pink-tracksuit girl came galloping over and stopped in front of us. Up close, I could see that she had a blue dolphin tattoo on her cheek (temporary, I hoped). "Can you tell her what the dolphin did today,

Clare?" the man asked her. The girl nodded vigorously: "He nearly touched Daddy's head!" I found this hard to visualize, but before I could ask for more details, the man had turned away and his daughter had climbed aboard the statue, shoving aside a boy who was riding Fungie's tail fin.

Behind the statue there was a stone building, its windows filled with Fungie posters and press clippings. I wandered over to read them. An eight-foot cardboard cutout of the dolphin reared up behind the glass: FUNGIE IS FINTASTIC! COME SEE HIM TODAY! INFO@DINGLEDOLPHIN.COM. A newspaper photo showed him rolling on his back next to a dinghy, while a woman leaned over the side to tickle his belly. DOLPHIN WHO JUST WANTS TO HAVE FUN, read the headline. So why had the "bighearted bottlenose" stayed in Dingle for so long? The writer had asked locals for their opinions. "Maybe he's just very sociable and likes the Irish way of life," one resident mused.

Another headline announced that "fun-loving Fungie the dolphin has somersaulted into the record books . . . as The Most Loyal Animal on the Planet!" To win this title, I read, Fungie had outdone a Risso's dolphin named Pelorus Jack, who spent twenty-four years, from 1888 to 1912, escorting ships through New Zealand's Cook Strait, a tricky passage between the North and South Islands. These waters are ferocious, full of submerged rocks, blasted by winds, and churned up by strong currents. Many boats had run into trouble there—until the dolphin arrived, and began to guide them safely across.

Pelorus Jack took this job seriously: he was very reliable. Usually he would just appear at the ship's bow; if he didn't immediately show up, boat captains would idle their engines and wait for him. For his navigational expertise and the joyful way he expressed himself—jumping across bow waves and rubbing against ships' hulls—the dolphin was beloved. "He swam alongside us in a kind of snuggling-up attitude," one seaman recalled.

By all accounts Pelorus Jack was a handsome animal, about fourteen feet long and colored a mottled silver, darker at the tips of his fins. As he got older, he turned white and his countless scrapes and scratches and scuffs stood out in relief. Like all Risso's dolphins he had a large round head and a tiny beak, giving him a wry, brainy appearance. Tourists flocked to see him. Songs were written about him. Sometimes he appeared in gossip columns.

When a passenger aboard a local ferry, the *Penguin*, shot at Pelorus Jack with a rifle, grazing him and causing him to disappear for weeks, the New Zealand government passed a law specifically to protect him. After his gunshot wound healed, the dolphin returned to his post. But, many witnesses claim, he never guided the *Penguin* again. If he happened to see that particular ferry he would dive immediately and vanish. In a twist of history that seems like karmic justice, three years after the incident the *Penguin* hit a rock and sank.

~~~~~~

The next morning I bought a ticket for the *Lady Avalon,* a sturdy blue-and-white trawler that departed at 9:00 a.m. for a Fungie tour of Dingle Bay. It was an overcast day, windless and soggy. I zipped up my raincoat and stood on the boat ramp near a sign that said WAIT BEHIND LINE FOR DOLPHIN FERRY. I had wondered if the weather would keep other dolphin-watchers at home, but the harbor was packed. Nobody seemed to even notice the drizzle.

When you consider the dolphin-based economy of Dingle, with its stores selling dolphin postcards and dolphin T-shirts and dolphin earrings, its art galleries full of dolphin paintings and dolphin drawings, its pizzerias serving Pizza Fungie—it is clear this is the town that Fungie built. According to Dingle's tourist bureau, three-quarters of all visitors come for one reason: to see its resident dolphin. During the summer, that adds up to about five thousand people per day. Including the *Lady Avalon,* there are nine dolphin ferries making multiple trips each day, seven days a week, an hour on the water with a money-back guarantee if Fungie does not appear.

A deckhand helped us aboard, and within minutes we were chugging slowly out of the harbor. Seabirds flew loops overhead. The water was a swampy olive color, flat as a bathtub, but when the light glanced off it a certain way it turned an upbeat slate blue. A dinghy and three sailboats circled in the center of the bay. The sailboats were tiny, barely big enough to hold two people; one of them had tomato-red sails that stood out like flags against the emerald fields and hills. I bent myself nearly double over the railing and stared down into the bay, but I saw nothing. If it were not for the knowledge that a large wild animal was hiding somewhere in here and he might pop up at any minute, this harbor circuit would easily qualify as the world's most boring boat ride.

"Anyone see him anywhere?" The captain, a man named Jimmy Flannery Sr., stuck his head out of the wheelhouse. No one had, but not because they weren't looking. People were crowded on top of one other with their cameras trained on the water. "Where is the dolphin?" a girl asked loudly. "Where is he, Mum?" Her mother lifted her up so she would have a better view. "Emily, you have to watch out," she said, "because the dolphin *is* out there somewhere."

Suddenly, from the stern, a lady in a yellow slicker

yelled: "There he is! Oh my gosh! I saw him!" With a whooshing outbreath the dolphin had surfaced, and he was close enough that I could see his distinctive face. Fungie looked tough, with white markings around his chin like an old man's whiskers. He bore noticeable scars: his beak was roughed up at the tip, and he was missing a chunk of his tail. On his throat he had the dolphin equivalent of deep wrinkles. I had read that Fungie was twelve feet long and weighed seven hundred pounds, but those numbers are low. This was a big, strong bottlenose. My first thought was that the Most Loyal Animal on the Planet could knock someone's lights out if he wanted to.

After following alongside us, Fungie dove, rocketing into the air seconds later next to the sailboats. He seemed especially fond of the boat with the red sails. Fungie stuck his head out of the water and splashed the sailors with enthusiasm. "It's sport for him," a bearded man in a checked cap said to me, nodding in Fungie's direction. "Rogue dolphin, he is. They leave their flock."

Watching the dolphin, I felt a glee, a doglike joy, emanating from him. No wonder the town had claimed him as their own—Fungie is as recognizable as any person. His face is as unique as yours or mine; in photographs it is obvious that he has aged over time. To see him is to know for sure that he is an individual with his own quirks and traits and habits, his own way of presenting himself in the world. There is absolutely no way the Dingle Chamber of Commerce could secretly swap in another dolphin as a substitute for Fungie, should he ever fail to report for boat-playing duty.

Once he'd arrived at our party Fungie was a skilled entertainer. He made perfect aerial flips and walked on his tail, and at one point he swam along on his back, clapping his pectoral fins. Many of his moves were surprisingly showy, less like natural behaviors than tricks he might have been taught in some lost chapter of his pre-Dingle life. Watching him, I found myself wondering if Fungie's past might have included a stint in captivity; if, back in the day, he had lived in a sea pen and somehow escaped. It had happened before, especially during storms. In Hurricane Katrina, for instance, eight dolphins from the Marine Life Oceanarium, in Gulfport, Mississippi, were swept from their pool by a thirty-foot storm surge, and landed in the Gulf of Mexico. Those dolphins ended up back in custody, but on occasion captives do get away. Unfortunately, they don't always know where to go or what to do with their sudden freedom, and so they seek out what they've become accustomed to: people. Could Fungie be a refugee?

We can only guess. Fungie's early life history has been erased by time and myth. Like every solitary dolphin, he comes with a built-in mystery: How did this happen? When, and why? Getting entangled in nets or fishing lines for a time, losing contact with his pod in rough seas, becoming orphaned or sick or injured for whatever reason— any of these situations might strand an individual dolphin, leaving him to fend for himself. Or maybe Fungie swam into this harbor, liked it, and simply decided to stay.

It was the Dingle fishermen who had noticed the dolphin first, and given him his name. Fungie trailed behind their boats as they returned to port, hoping, no doubt, for a handout of fish, but probably also yearning for company. At sunset he could often be seen jumping in the center of the bay, framed in silhouette like a dolphin on a movie poster. Sometimes, as if to show his gratitude or establish himself as a thoughtful neighbor, Fungie would catch salmon and trout, and toss them into boats.

Three years into his Dingle residency the dolphin got some swimming companions. Sheila Stokes and Brian Holmes, a couple from nearby Cork, showed up in thick wet suits, slipped into the water, and began to snorkel with him. For weeks Fungie kept his distance, but Stokes and Holmes were persistent, spending hours in the frigid bay. They were respectful, too, letting the dolphin be the one to initiate contact. Their patience paid off: Fungie began to brush against Stokes's outstretched hand. "You could sense his excitement, as well as my own," Stokes said, "because he went off and did a few leaps and flips in the bay before coming back for more touching. And from then on, he let us touch him a lot of the time." While Stokes rubbed Fungie's fins and belly, and ran her hands over his beak and his head, Holmes shot video of the dolphin looking as moony as a high school kid with a crush.

Pictures of Fungie trickled out, followed by some local press. Soon a steady stream of people flowed into Dingle, eager to have their own dolphin encounters. Fungie handled this pretty well, allowing people to approach him. He had his favorites, certain swimmers or kayaks or boats that he preferred, though whenever Stokes showed up, it was as if no one else existed. The bay filled with sailors and snorkelers and diving groups, kids bobbing in life jackets, teenagers riding Jet Skis, people rattling anchor chains and towing boogie boards to get the dolphin's attention. Usually, Fungie responded to chaos or obnoxious behavior by swimming off, but one time he rammed a German tourist in the groin, an injury that sent the man to the hospital.

By this time, with all the dolphin-watching boats circling the harbor, the swimmers had mostly given up. In any case, Fungie seemed to appreciate speed. When Flannery opened the *Lady Avalon*'s throttle, the dolphin veered away from the red sailboat and began to porpoise alongside us, jumping as high as the railings. "Wahhhhhh!" yelled a boy, as Fungie burst out of the water only inches away. By now our hour was almost up; it was as though Flannery and Fungie had planned this series of leaps as a grand finale. It could not have been executed any better if it had been part of a Las Vegas show.

Back at the docks, I asked Flannery which of Fungie's tricks was the most impressive, whether the dolphin had ever amazed him with some new move. The captain scratched his head and nodded: "He does a backflip. Comes clear out of the water."

I decided to share my theory about Fungie's past, not realizing that by doing so I was questioning the town's most sacred legend. "It seems like someone must have trained him," I said. "Do you know if they did?" Flannery, who had been smiling pleasantly enough before I said this, turned and stared at me hard. A shadow passed over his face, darkening it like a thundercloud. "Not at all," he said curtly, turning away dismissively. "He is a totally wild animal."

Dolly in France and Paquito in Spain; Egypt's Olin, who befriended a tribe of Bedouins in the Gulf of Aqaba; Charlie-Bubbles from Newfoundland; Springer from

Seattle; Scar from New Zealand; Chas, who loved a particular buoy in the Thames river—these and so many other solitary dolphins have made themselves known to us. That is usually where the problems begin.

The relationship between a solitary dolphin and the people who want to see him worries biologists, who fear—correctly—that these encounters will end badly for the dolphin. In this case, Fungie is an exception, having far exceeded the life expectancy for a wild bottlenose who interacts daily with humans. Sadly, most friendly solitary dolphins don't last for nearly as long. Their biggest threat, by far, is propellers, which seem as interesting to curious dolphins as they are deadly: scientists have heard dolphins playfully mimicking the sounds of motorboat engines underwater, the way kids do with their favorite toy trucks.

Wilma and Echo, orphan belugas from Nova Scotia, Canada, both died from being hit by propellers, but not before charming thousands of people, gliding up to sightseeing boats to let passengers stroke their skin. Jet, a bottle-nose from the Isle of Wight, in England, had his tail chopped off by a propeller and bled to death. Freddie, another British bottlenose whose companion had swallowed a plastic bag and washed up dead on the beach, liked to swim upside down beneath motorized dinghies; he also enjoyed the flume of a sewage outtake pipe. Both were dangerous attractions. The chemical-treated waste infected Freddie's skin, turning it a grizzled gray, but once again, it was a propeller that got him. Luna, a beautiful lone orca calf who lived near a marina in Nootka Sound, British Columbia, was the subject of a movie, *The Whale*, narrated by Scarlett Johansson. He survived for five years before being hit by a tugboat.

But propellers are only one hazard among many. Over in Israel, Dobbie, a bottlenose who loved to play with the air bubbles from scuba divers, washed up on shore full of bullet holes. In Australia, Zero Three, a young male bottlenose, was poisoned by toxic chemicals that were dumped in the river where he swam. A French bottlenose named Jean Floc'h paid for his fascination with rowboats; he was beaten to death with wooden oars. Dolphins who gravitated toward us have also been stabbed with knives and screwdrivers and even ballpoint pens, strangled by wire and fishing line, shot by spearguns, targeted with explosives, and purposely run over by Jet Skis.

Surrounded by people who want to swim with them, touch them, and grab their fins, dolphins can become aggressive themselves. Solitary dolphins, removed from everything familiar and confused by their new acquaintances, have pinned snorkelers to the seafloor, and clubbed swimmers with their tails. Far from rescuing people, if a

dolphin is angry enough he might prevent them from exit-
ing the water, or push them farther out to sea.

~~~~~~

The one thing we know for sure about lone friendly dolphins is that we are likely to meet more of them. A 2008
global count of wild dolphins who have sought human
company shows a dramatic rise in their numbers since
1980. Across the world, it seems, the dolphins' society and
ours are colliding.

When you think about it, this culture clash is inevi-
table. A wild dolphin doesn't end up with a Twitter account
unless something has gone very wrong before that, and the
oceans these days are a mad mess of trouble. Even if dolphins manage to avoid our web of fishing nets and longlines, they still must deal with endless pollution, oil spills,
habitat destruction, food depletion, man-made underwater
noise—the list goes on. Of course we'll find dolphins
among us: they have nowhere else to go.

In so many ways, I realized, Dingle is a best-case sce-
nario for a pod-less dolphin. When you watch Fungie, you
can plainly see that he is having fun. He hunts for his own
food. He is savvy enough to avoid propellers and discern-
ing enough to dodge anyone who might harm him. He has

bonded with people, but he's not completely isolated from his own species: at times, other dolphins venture into the bay. Lately, Fungie had been seen playing with two female bottlenoses, the three of them leaping together and appearing to embrace one another. In all situations the town protects his interests: what's good for Fungie is good for them. And if the Most Loyal Animal on the Planet ever decides that he has been loyal to Dingle for long enough, he is free to leave whenever he pleases.

Obviously, the town is praying that never happens. In 2013, to mark the dolphin's thirtieth anniversary as a citizen, Dingle threw a three-day party, the Fungie Festival. Reading the schedule, I almost fell over in delight. Events included art and photo exhibitions (images of Fungie), poetry readings (works inspired by Fungie), concerts (music written for Fungie), historical lectures ("Fungie: The Early Years"), scientific talks ("Fungie and Other Solitary Dolphins Around the World"), children's book readings (a series starring Fungie), conversation circles (people talking about how Fungie has affected their lives)—plus morning swims, evening swims, and a boat trip to bless the dolphin "out of gratitude for all he offers so freely to people and to celebrate his presence at the mouth of the harbor."

As I drove away from Dingle, the bay shining behind me, I gave my own silent thanks to the people who had cared enough to protect a lone dolphin, the town with a Fungie-shaped space in its heart. The dolphin has repaid them, and then some. It's an uncommon relationship and beautiful to see. I planned to keep the Fungie Festival, all the brightness of that gathering, in the front row of my mind: I knew I would need it as a touchstone. The next place I planned to visit was also a pretty little fishing town. It, too, had dolphins. There, as well, dolphins played a major role in local affairs.

But instead of being a haven for the animals, this town had chosen differently.

Chapter 5

Welcome to Taiji

≈≈≈≈

"**O**kay now. We've just been told that we need to go directly to the police station for processing." Mark Palmer stood at the front of the bus to address us. He was sweating and smiling. I liked Palmer's voice. It was deep, reassuring, and cheerful, even though we were probably headed into trouble. Actually, I liked everything about Palmer—and his colleague Mark Berman and everyone else aboard this tour bus. We were driving through the mountains and along the curvy roads of southeastern Japan, rolling toward our destination: the notorious dolphin-hunting town of Taiji. What I didn't like was the idea of heading straight to the police station when we got there.

In the Oscar-winning documentary *The Cove*, viewers

have seen what happens in Taiji. This pretty seaside town is up to some very ugly business: catching, killing, and selling dolphins. Before they hunted dolphins, the Taiji fishermen hunted whales. Taiji's whaling history dates back centuries, to 1675, but its dolphin hunt, which began in 1969, is relatively new. It is also horrible. All over the world, people have protested loudly against it. Because of this, the town is nasty to outsiders. In the movie, *The Cove*'s main character, American dolphin activist Ric O'Barry, is followed, yelled at, thrown out of public places, and threatened whenever he shows up in Taiji. O'Barry believes the dolphin hunters would actually kill him if they thought they could get away with it.

O'Barry, now seventy-eight years old, has a unique background: he trained Flipper, the most famous dolphin in the world. Throughout the 1960s, O'Barry taught the five female bottlenose dolphins who played Flipper to perform the amazing feats that made the TV show such a hit. Before that, he collected wild dolphins for the Miami Seaquarium, scooping up more than a hundred animals around Florida and the Bahamas. O'Barry caught dolphins for captivity and looked after captive dolphins and trained captive dolphins, and he lived large while he was doing it, cruising around Miami in a Porsche, entertaining celebrities who dropped by to hang out with Flipper, earning a hefty salary. There was only one problem: "About half-way through the TV series I really started having second thoughts about dolphin captivity," he says. "But I didn't actually do anything. Things were going too well to ruin the party." That changed in 1970, when his favorite Flipper dolphin, Kathy, died in his arms, looking up at him and simply refusing to take another breath. "She was really depressed," O'Barry recalled. "I could feel it. I could see it." He believed the dolphin had committed suicide. The next day, O'Barry switched careers. For the past forty-five years he has dedicated his life to dolphin welfare, traveling all over the world doing everything he can to help them.

It was O'Barry who had invited me to Taiji. Each year on September 1, opening day of Japan's seven-month dolphin-hunting season, O'Barry and his group, the Dolphin Project, gather in the cove to protest, and then every day after that they track the hunters' movements, filming everything that occurs and broadcasting it on the Internet. "I will keep returning to Taiji until they stop or I drop," O'Barry told me. I had instantly agreed to come, though I knew the trip would be disturbing. I felt it was important to see what was happening at the cove with my own eyes.

I flew to Osaka, Japan, on August 30 to meet the group; O'Barry would be joining us two days later, in Taiji. The bus ride from Osaka to Taiji lasted six hours. Our group included about thirty activists, mostly in their twenties and thirties, three translators, plus Palmer and Berman. Both men were associate directors of Earth Island Institute, the environmental group from Berkeley, California, that supported O'Barry's work.

Through the bus windows I could see a hillside of closely packed houses with brown and beige roofs, somber earth tones rather than happy seaside colors. We drove by a tsunami warning sign, a yellow triangle filled with threatening black waves, and then we crossed over a bridge that was topped by a small dolphin statue. The dolphin's mouth was open as though he were yelling for help.

In general, Japan and other nations disagree about whether *any* cetaceans deserve protection. Japanese fisheries officials have openly described killing dolphins and whales as a public service; one spokesman referred to them as "the cockroaches of the sea." They believe, wrongly, that if there are fewer dolphins and whales there will be more fish left for humans to eat. But the ocean is more complicated than that, and removing predators from its waters disrupts an intricate balance. Cetaceans are vital members of the marine ecosystem, and they play an essential role in creating healthy fish populations. Without them, we would be in deep trouble.

Whale and dolphin meat is illegal to eat in most countries because of the animals' endangered status, but in Japan it is eaten by many people, and served widely in restaurants. Taiji is proud of its whale-hunting history, and one of the first things you see when you drive into the town is a massive whaling ship, the *Kyo Maru I*. To me, it was a disturbing sight, a haunting reminder that we almost harpooned the great whales out of existence. I looked past it and saw the Pacific Ocean, calm and glassy in the early evening light, and then we rounded one last corner and the cove lay in front of us.

It was smaller than it had looked in the movie, maybe two hundred yards long and sixty yards across, U-shaped and rocky, flanked on both sides by steep, thickly forested hills. From the road you could look down on the cove's pebbly beach and into its shallow green waters. The place was eerily still, without even a breath of wind. The streets were empty. The seaside walkways were blocked by heavy chain-link and barbed-wire fencing with signs that said NO TRESPASSING. DANGER. WATCH FOR FALLING ROCK and THIS IS A RESTRICTED AREA. At the cove there were no children playing with toy boats, no Frisbee-chasing dogs, no summer ice cream carts, no couples enjoying the sunset. The only other people I could see were policemen, about forty of them, standing across the street in front of their police station. The station is located at the cove for a specific reason: to convince people like us that it isn't a good idea to protest there.

Our bus driver turned into a parking lot and stopped beside some lonely-looking palm trees. Though it was quiet around here today, that wouldn't be true tomorrow. I knew that confrontations between dolphin activists and dolphin hunters could get heated, and each year more people kept showing up on September 1 to protest at the cove. In recent years, Japanese nationalists and yakuza (Japanese gangsters) had shown up, too. They threatened and harassed anyone who wanted to raise their voice against the dolphin hunt. Dolphin protesters had been followed through Taiji's streets; the yakuza had also tried to shove a woman from the environmental group Sea Shepherd into a van, in what seemed like an attempt to abduct her. As a result of the rising tensions, many Japanese federal policemen patrolled Taiji. O'Barry's groups always behaved peacefully and obeyed all the laws, but even so, the police wanted to interview us and register our passports before we could check in to our hotel.

Palmer stood up again. "We'll go in two at a time," he said as the bus doors opened.

"Be pleasant." He chuckled drily. "And remember, if you don't understand what they're saying, just smile and nod."

"I ask you some questions so please." The policeman was brisk and polite. He sat at a small desk wearing a neat navy uniform. His English wasn't great, but we understood one another. Opening my passport, he examined it for several minutes, making careful notes as he flipped through its pages. After a while he handed it to another policeman sitting next to him. The two men began to speak in Japanese. I smiled and nodded.

The first policeman turned back to me. "What are you doing here?" he asked.

"Uh . . ." Was there a right answer? "I'm here to learn."

"Ohhhhhhh."

"I observe."

"Mmmmmm. Demonstration is here tomorrow. Do you take part in this?"

"Yes."

"Oh oh oh oh oh. Tell me about one thing. Have you ever heard of the conflict right-wing nationalists?"

"I heard something."

"They are waiting in the next town," he said, shaking his head and looking grave. "They can be dangerous. They are gonna come here tomorrow, many. Say bad things. So please be careful."

"I will. I will be careful."

"Please ignore.

"I will, definitely."

"And don't push anyone."

"No, no. I don't push."

He handed back my passport and motioned for the next person to come in. Nodding goodbye, I went outside to join the others. Veronica, a graceful woman from Bolivia who had traveled here with her daughter, was staring at the cove, crying. Two Australian girls, Yaz and Britt, both nineteen-year-olds from Perth, stood next to her. "I can't take it all in," Britt said, looking upset. She had experience with tough situations: at fourteen, she had saved up her money and flown to Nepal to work at Mother Teresa's mission.

It was impossible for any of us to forget that tens of thousands of dolphins had been killed on this spot, in the cruelest possible way. The hunters use sound to drive the dolphins toward the shore, banging on metal poles and creating a wall of noise that disorients and terrifies the dolphins. After the pods are driven into the cove, they are often left in there for days without food or fresh water. (Like us, dolphins can't hydrate with salt water; they extract fresh water from the fish they catch.) When a slaughter begins, the pod can hear one another's cries. As their friends and families are killed nearby, the dolphins know exactly what is going on. Every fact about the dolphin hunt in Taiji made clear that it needed to be stopped. But how could we make this happen?

After the police finished questioning us, we drove to the Kayu hotel. We were spending a single night at this hotel. For the rest of the week we would stay in Kii-Katsuura, the neighboring town, five minutes away. As our luggage was unloaded, I asked Berman why we had to move. He grimaced. "Staying in Taiji is really not fun," he said. "They don't like us here. They'll take our money, but they really don't like us."

"Oh, they don't like us at *all*," a slender blond woman standing next to him added. "Kii-Katsuura is bigger and the hotel there has better security."

The woman's name was Carrie Burns, and she spoke from experience. Carrie and her husband, Tim, had been coming to Taiji for the past three years, flying from their home in St. Petersburg, Florida. Like everyone else in the group, they were inspired to come here after seeing *The Cove*. Once they decided to get involved, the Burnses had jumped in with both feet. Carrie learned everything she possibly could about the dolphin hunt. Tim ran O'Barry's Cove Monitor program, making sure that each morning at dawn, when the dolphin-hunting boats left the harbor, someone was perched at a hillside lookout with binoculars and a camera. Whenever the hunters chased dolphins into the cove, the cove monitors took pictures and video,

81

counted the captured animals, watched everything that was happening, and then broadcast it all through social media.

As images appeared in the news of the cove's water stained red with blood, of fishermen killing dolphins with spears and knives, of dolphin trainers wading in to select the youngest and prettiest dolphins to be shipped off to marine parks—as the outside world began to see what was going on in this place—the town had attempted to cut off the sight lines. They put up barricades, blocked paths, and obscured the water with huge tarps, but there were still a few vantage points left. None of them were ideal or easy to get to, and often the monitors would show up at a formerly accessible spot only to find it suddenly closed, fenced off and under guard.

Despite all the obstacles, the monitors persisted, and they always found a way to film what was going on in the cove. But their work was difficult. Watching hundreds of dolphins fight for their lives—and lose—took a toll on their emotions.

Palmer had asked us to drop off our bags in our rooms and then meet in his room to discuss tomorrow's schedule. Walking through the hotel hallways felt creepy, as though I were being watched by hidden cameras. When I arrived at Palmer's doorway, I ducked in, relieved. Everyone was gathered around, sitting on the floor. "All right," Palmer said, quieting us.

At sixty-one years old, Palmer had spent his career helping the environment. He had founded and led the Endangered Species Committee of California, and served as a chairman for one of the country's most powerful conservation groups, the Sierra Club. For decades he had worked to save wild animals and wild places in countless ways, in his own relaxed, humor-filled, get-it-done style.

"Let's begin with the subject of danger," he said. "Apparently there are extreme groups here—the police should keep them away from us. You don't want to go near them. By all means, do not get into a shoving match. There is always the possibility that you will be arrested along with the guy who was shoving you."

Getting arrested, we all knew, was a bad idea in Japan. You could be held in jail for a month without being charged, and you would definitely be kicked out of the country and not allowed to return. While it is tempting to cut the nets in the cove or otherwise interfere with Taiji's dolphin hunters, the main reason O'Barry doesn't recommend doing this is because it doesn't work. In his emails to his followers, he stressed the importance of restrained, respectful behavior. Over the years, he'd seen that fighting with the hunters only made them more determined to keep killing dolphins.

Instead, he takes a different approach. He points out a disturbing fact: that eating dolphin meat is about as healthy as eating hazardous waste.

Some of the worst pollutants accumulate in dolphins' fatty flesh, including mercury, a potent neurotoxin. When even low levels of mercury enter your body, it causes memory loss, nerve tremors, heart attacks, liver failure, loss of hair, teeth, and nails, blurred vision, impaired hearing, muscle weakness, high blood pressure, insomnia, and a horrible syndrome called desquamation, which is basically your skin peeling off. If you ingest even tiny doses of mercury, the toxin stays in your system and its effects grow worse over time.

When dolphin meat purchased in Taiji supermarkets—and served nationwide in school lunches—was proven to be full of mercury in 2002, the Japanese media ignored this news. In 2008, after tests of Taiji residents showed sharply elevated mercury levels in their bodies, enough to cause brain damage and birth defects, again the press was silent. Two town councilmen, Hisato Ryono and Junichiro Yamashita, were so alarmed by this news that they paid out of their own pockets to print flyers informing people about the perils of eating dolphin. "This is a small town, where people are afraid to speak out," Yamashita said. "But we can't sit silent about a health problem like this."

This was a critical health issue for Japan. Throughout the country, people were eating dolphin and whale meat so polluted that it was poisonous—one sample was found to contain five thousand times the limit for mercury contamination; another gave rats kidney failure after a single mouthful. But the Japanese government has issued no warnings, other than advising children and pregnant women to eat it in moderation. "There is a real danger in whale and dolphin meat, but word is not getting out," researcher Tetsuya Endo from the University of Hokkaido, whose lab did many of the tests, told the *New York Times*.

Despite this, the Taiji Fishermen's Union, the town's mayor, and the Japanese government continue to insist that the meat is safe to eat. Tomorrow our main job was to contradict them, standing at the cove holding signs that said in Japanese: DOLPHIN MEAT IS CONTAMINATED WITH MERCURY.

"So let's head out and get some actual sleep," Palmer said, wrapping things up. "You should be down in the lobby at ten a.m., checked out with your luggage." The police had advised that we not leave the hotel before that, he told us, but then added: "I think it's okay if you're not alone. Stay in groups, stay in lighted areas." I looked around the room. Nobody looked all that eager to head out into the streets of Taiji.

"GO HOME! GO HOME! YOU GO HOME!"

The young man stood in front of me with his fists clenched, screaming so hard that every tendon in his neck was visible. He wore a hat and big sunglasses, a baggy black T-shirt, and pants pulled so low they were almost falling off. He was small and wiry and about as angry as any person I'd ever seen. With him were a few dozen of his friends. They were angry, too; one guy was even holding up a sign that said, in bold letters: ANGRY! I was relieved to see that behind them a line of police stood, holding their batons with crisp white gloves.

We had stepped off the bus into this crowd, the noise and fury hitting us like a wall. The day was hazy, damp with humidity and broiling with heat. It had to be at least a hundred degrees out. The sun flared through the clouds, bleaching the sky to white. For a moment, I felt dizzy.

To get down to the cove, we had to walk by a group of nationalists who had lined both sides of the road, shaking Japanese flags and yelling at us. The police surrounded us as we walked. The officers were professional and seemed genuinely interested in protecting us. Two black sedans drove by slowly with loudspeakers on their roofs, blaring more insults.

We made our way to the rocky beach, trailing policemen. The nationalists and assorted angry people stayed
bunched on the roadway above. A pair of coast guard boats
floated offshore, ready for potential trouble on the water.
A crowd of cameramen and reporters were already down
at the cove, and they surged toward us. "Smile and look
happy!" Berman instructed.

Palmer, at the front of our group, stopped at the edge
of the beach. One of the cameramen thrust a microphone
at him. "We'll have a series of events now," Palmer said,
"starting first with a circle for the dolphins. A moment of
silence—a prayer, if you will. For the dolphins who have
died here in Taiji, and the dolphins who will die this year."
He paused for a long beat. "We also wish to have a prayer
for the people of Japan. Many died, as you know, during the
earthquake and tsunami in March 2011. Today we honor
the souls of the dolphins and the souls of the people."

Palmer's voice was warm but unemotional. It was the
voice of reason, of hope that one day instead of anger at
the cove there might be productive communication. Part
of O'Barry's plan to end the dolphin hunt involved helping
the fishermen develop ecotourism options. Taiji's coastline is stunning, and the cove itself is part of a national
park that could obviously be put to better use than as a
crude slaughterhouse.

Economically, dolphin watching would seem to make far better sense than dolphin hunting: not many people want to eat the mercury-laden dolphin meat, and it sells for only six dollars a pound. But there is another financial incentive for the hunters to continue driving dolphins into the cove, and it's Taiji's dirtiest secret: the town itself is the biggest trafficker of live dolphins in the world.

While a dead dolphin is worth maybe five hundred dollars to the Taiji Fishermen's Union, a live dolphin—especially a young female—can be sold to a marine park for more than $150,000. About 10 percent of the dolphins driven into the cove are sold live, bringing in millions of dollars. In 2012, for instance, marine parks bought 156 bottlenoses, 49 spotted dolphins, 2 pilot whales, 14 Risso's dolphins, 2 striped dolphins, and 24 white-sided dolphins from Taiji. These dolphins were shipped to all corners of Japan, and also to Korea, China, Vietnam, Russia, and the Ukraine, among other places.

Within a mile of where we were standing there were at least four dolphin-brokering businesses, each with its own trainers. After their capture, the animals were moved into holding pens and dingy concrete pools at one of these places and taught some basic tricks, which increased their market value. As a result, Taiji is a one-stop-shopping destination for anyone who would like to buy a dolphin, and who doesn't mind plucking that dolphin out of a pool of blood that contains the dead bodies of his entire family.

We joined hands for our moment of silence, while above us on the road, people continued to yell. The quieter we were, the angrier they became.

For the first time in a decade, since O'Barry had been coming to protest at the cove, his group this year included a dozen Japanese citizens. This counted as excellent progress. In Japan it is considered impolite to argue—to disagree with other people in your opinions or your actions. So for a citizen to publicly protest the dolphin hunt was a real act of bravery. I admired all the people I met who were willing to stand up for what they believed in, even when that was not an easy thing to do. And nothing about this situation was easy.

〰〰〰

Ric O'Barry arrived the next morning. I caught up with him in front of our second hotel. The hotel's architecture reminded me of a cruise ship, but it was more than a mile long. The ocean lapped on its doorstep. Small ferries decorated to look like dolphins and whales—with tail fins and googly cartoon eyes—transported guests from its front door to the main streets of Kii-Katsuura, the town next door to Taiji.

Though he had flown for thirteen hours, been questioned by officials for four hours in the Tokyo airport, and then driven seven hours to get here, O'Barry took the time to give a press conference before he'd even checked in to his room. He stood on the street speaking to some Japanese reporters, wearing a blue hoodie, gray hiking pants, and flip-flops, hiding his tired eyes behind Ray-Ban sunglasses. His white hair strayed out from under a khaki baseball cap. "What do you . . . um . . . what is your wish, what do you want the fishermen in Taiji . . . ?" asked a man with glasses, holding a notebook.

"To stop killing the dolphins," O'Barry said, with a frown. "It's really simple."

No matter how sleep-deprived, O'Barry is a lively interview subject and an excellent debater. He is plainspoken and direct and he delivers his message in calm, deliberate tones, with frequent jabs of humor. He is a master at pointing out the absurdities and hypocrisies of marine parks: "We love our dolphins like they're our family—I hear that a lot. Really? You lock your family in a room and force them to do tricks before they eat their dinner?"

While O'Barry took a nap for his jet lag, Berman and I decided to drive back into Taiji. We wanted to visit the Taiji Whale Museum, located next to the cove. The museum's name is misleading: it is actually a *whaling* museum, showcasing Japan's history of hunting whales and dolphins. The museum also contains an aquarium and a sea pen stocked with exotic dolphin species, all of whom were captured at the cove.

Berman and I took a taxi to Taiji, getting out in front of the museum. Masako Maxwell, a Japanese American woman from Los Angeles who devoted herself to helping animals of every species, came along with us, too. Maxwell had a ponytail down to her waist and tattoos on her arms, and she carried herself with a quiet strength. She didn't have to make a lot of noise—she just got things done. "I was born and raised in Japan, and I feel it's my mission to come here and be useful," she said when we met. As a tech expert, Maxwell ran O'Barry's Japanese website and social media. "She's key to getting our information out to the people of Japan," Palmer had told me.

For Berman and me, Maxwell was also key to our chances of getting into the museum. Far from being a neutral educational or scientific facility, removed from the controversy and carnage that was going on at the cove, the Taiji Whale Museum was the town's main dolphin trafficker.

Alongside tanks that housed its performing dolphins were additional floating pens that contained dolphins for sale. Although it is a public building, its ticket windows were filled with signs saying: NO ANTI-WHALERS ARE ALLOWED INSIDE THE MUSEUM.

You might wonder how the cashiers would decide who could come in and who could not. Was there a secret handshake, known only to fans of the dolphin hunt? In the end, the Taiji Whale Museum had decided to simply refuse admission to anyone who wasn't Japanese (even though that is illegal). Usually, though, if a Westerner could get his hands on a ticket he could get past the door—unless he seemed likely to cause trouble.

Maxwell went to buy the tickets while Berman and I waited, out of sight. I looked down and noticed that I was standing on a ceramic tile painted with dolphins. Everywhere you turned in this town, there were cetaceans. Whales were plastered on buildings; dolphins were painted on signs. WE LOVE DOLPHINS! one road sign exclaimed. It didn't seem like Taiji could get any weirder, but then Maxwell appeared with the tickets, Berman and I pulled on our hats and sunglasses and made our way into the museum, and I realized that every strange experience I'd had until now was only a warm-up for this.

Inside, four whale skeletons hung from the ceiling. A

model of a live whale dangled up there, too, pursued by a life-size boat filled with a dozen men hurling spears. Below, there was a puppet show depicting how the animals were killed: you could press a button and watch boats attack a whale that popped up from a hole. Harpoons of all shapes and sizes were displayed, along with maps of celebrated whale-hunting grounds. But if the first floor was a history lesson, the second floor was all about biology.

The first thing I saw at the top of the stairs was a glass case that contained the head of a striped dolphin. The head was pinkish, suspended in pale yellow liquid. His eyes were open, which made it look disturbingly alive. The dolphin was smiling, as all dolphins do, proving once and for all that this feature of their anatomy does not mean they are always happy. Lined up near the head were four cylinders filled with dolphin calves in various stages of development. They were squashed in, so their tails curled under their tiny bodies. I was startled to see that their fledgling fins looked exactly like arms.

The whole floor was a gallery of specimens: a floating bottlenose brain, a pickled humpback whale embryo, tissuey slices of . . . something. Maxwell walked down the row, reading off the contents of glass bottles and jars: "Whale heart, whale tongue, whale spleen. And, oh! This one is an orca."

It was hard not to be shocked by the sight of a killer whale calf lying on its side in a liquid-filled case. You could just barely make out his coloration, a whisper of difference where black met white. The orca's small body was so smooth it glistened. Looking at it, Berman let out a long breath, shook his head, and walked away.

We retreated downstairs and through the gift shop, past the freezer filled with dolphin and whale meat, the cans of dolphin stew stacked next to the dolphin stuffed toys and T-shirts and key chains. Outside, loud music signaled the start of the dolphin show. We sat down at the top of the bleachers so we could watch the audience as well as the show. The crowd consisted mostly of families with screaming toddlers.

A squad of six trainers took up their positions—young women in tangerine polo shirts and navy Bermuda shorts—and the show began in a sea pen that looked like the cove, except this one was separated from the open ocean by a thick cement barrier. There was no tidal flow in here, no exchange of fresh seawater with the waves, no fish. The enclosure was still and stagnant and hot. One of the trainers blew her whistle and a Risso's dolphin leaped out of the water, followed by a pilot whale who had to be fifteen feet long. A third huge dolphin flipped onto his back and began to swim by us, waving his pectoral fins. Berman looked depressed. "That's a false killer whale," he said. "A very pelagic deepwater animal. He won't last long here."

I was still stuck on the Risso's dolphin. He was the most unusual dolphin I'd ever seen, his gray-blue body covered in fantastic scribbles. He looked like an adorable alien. Actually, they all did. The pilot whale's jet-black head was almost perfectly round; the false killer whale still bore traces of the dolphin's earliest incarnation as a sleek, wolfish creature. All three dolphins were magnificent, absolute marvels of the ocean, and by all rights they should have been out in the Pacific, doing what fifty-five million years of evolution had designed them to do in the most important ecosystem on earth, instead of in here, performing tricks to the beat of cheesy pop songs.

As I watched, sweat trickled down the back of my neck, but something else was rising: anger. The show was soul-crushingly stupid. All of this was stupid, everything that went on at the cove, the entire arrogant, selfish relationship we had with these animals and with all of nature, as though these creatures existed only for our purposes. We behaved as though we were gods, deciding the fate of everything. But we weren't. We were just dumb. I felt a wave of sadness wash over me.

The performance ended. I was in a dark mood and would have loved to leave, but Berman wanted to check on the bottlenoses in the indoor tanks. They were in a circular white building at the far end of the sea pen. Inside, it reeked of chlorine. Three bottlenoses were crammed in a shallow tank that arched over a walkway, its windows dirty and cloudy and scratched. One dolphin swam up to Berman and stopped in front of him, looking him directly in the eye. Berman touched his hand to the plexiglass. "You want to go home, don't you, buddy?" he said softly.

The walkway ended in a murky aquarium, lit by buzzing fluorescent lights. One shoebox-size tank contained three spotted porcupine fish, a species I especially love, and as I watched them fluttering hopelessly my mood sank further. No effort had been made to include coral or any kind of ocean features; an electrical cord encased in plastic was the tank's only decoration.

Depressed, we headed for the exit, and passed a trainer feeding the false killer whale and the pilot whale. The animals spyhopped in front of her, poking their heads out of the water with their mouths open. The trainer had short hair and a cheery round face. She was young, perhaps still a teenager. "Hello," she said.

"Oh, do you speak English?" Berman said, stopping abruptly. "Can I ask you a few questions?"

The girl examined Maxwell warily and replied in Japanese.

"She won't let you take video," Maxwell translated, "but you can ask her some questions."

"You know they hunt dolphins here?" Berman asked, wasting no time.

The girl paused. "Yeah," she said.

Berman looked at her. "So do you feel sympathy? For those dolphins?"

The girl stared back at him. She puffed out her cheeks and crinkled her nose. "Mmmmmmmmmmm," she said, moving the air from one cheek to the other. "Mmmmmm." She seemed to do this for about ten minutes. "Sympathy?" she said finally, then spat it out sharply: "NO."

Maxwell and I glanced at one another. A security guard, noticing the conversation, was walking quickly toward us.

"I'm just asking your personal opinion," Berman pressed. "Not the opinion of this place."

The girl inflated her cheeks again. "I'm not feeling sympathy because sometimes people hunting deer and they are hunting . . . cow or something. And I can't recognize what's the difference." She pointed to the false killer whale and the pilot whale, who were staring so intently at us from such a close distance that they seemed to be part of the conversation. "I know it's really intelligent," she said, with a shrug. "But I feel that cows are also really intelligent and we are willing to eat them, so . . ."

The security guard was upon us. He didn't seem pleased. "Whale-as! Whale-as!" he barked, making a shooing gesture. Rather than argue with him, we left.

It wasn't the first time I'd heard someone defend the dolphin hunt by accusing others of similar mistreatment of animals. But if the point of the hunt is to get food, then simultaneously selling the animals for hundreds of thousands of dollars is impossible to justify. If dolphins are extremely valuable, then how can they also be completely dispensable? Not to mention that when we kill *any* creature for food we have ethical obligations: to do a clean, swift job of it, to avoid taking endangered species, to show respect and gratitude always, to tread as lightly as possible on the balance of life in an environment. None of these things were happening in Taiji.

~~~~~

O'Barry and I met in the lobby that afternoon. The hotel's ground floor reminded me of an airport terminal, if every traveler who passed through it were wearing a *yukata*— a kimono-like cotton bathrobe—and rubber flip-flops. There were at least twenty hot spring baths sprinkled throughout the property, so many buildings and wings and tunnels and corridors that if you weren't armed with a map you could be lost for days. As a helpful guide, the hotel had painted colored lines on the floor: take green for the cave baths, orange for the lava-rock baths, red for the cedar baths.

I hadn't eaten in a while—the combination of stress, heat, and furious conflict is not very appetizing—so we decided to have lunch at a restaurant O'Barry liked in Kii-Katsuura. As we crossed the street, a car caught my eye. It was a black Infinity sedan, parked between two buildings. Yesterday I'd seen it cruising around at the cove. The men in the car were yakuza, Palmer had pointed out, part of Japan's organized crime. They tended to insert themselves into highly profitable industries, and dolphin trafficking qualified. I had noticed the Infinity as we'd exited the bus—it stood out among the battered loudspeaker vans—and I'd gotten a close look at the men inside it. They were dressed differently than the nationalists: instead of T-shirts and polyester track pants, they wore hipster sunglasses and understated dark clothes. They all had shaved heads. Even the police had avoided them.

"Hey," I said, nudging O'Barry. "I think those guys were at the cove yesterday." The two men sat in the front seats eyeing us coldly. When you describe someone as "a person you wouldn't want to meet in a dark alley," these were the type of people you meant—and here they were right now, in a dark alley.

O'Barry turned to look. "I know him," he said, pointing

to the man in the passenger seat. "Last year that guy threatened to kill me on camera. I'll send you the footage. He is screaming into the camera, 'I'm gonna kill you, O'Barry! I kill you!' Oh yeah, he's a yakuza."

"He seems pretty scary," I said.

"He's a nutjob!" O'Barry studied the car. "That's why I'm a little afraid of him, because with these guys—you know, anything could happen."

I was disturbed by the fact that professional criminals had followed us to our hotel, but O'Barry seemed to take it in stride. For him, being menaced was part of the job. "If you can get a dolphin in the right place, you can make a million dollars a year off that one dolphin," he has pointed out. The fact that marine parks make a lot of money from their dolphin shows exposes him to all kinds of dangers when he shows up, wanting to set their dolphins free.

Not long ago in Indonesia, O'Barry had been advised by police to wear a bulletproof vest after he had successfully shut down a traveling circus that featured dolphins jumping through hoops of fire. Later during that same trip, he awoke in the night to the sounds of someone trying to break open his hotel room door. While it is never easy to take dolphins away from people who profit from them, some situations are more perilous than others. O'Barry had recently been told about a desperate situation involving two dolphins who had been shipped into the mountains of Turkey, and he planned to go there soon to see what he could do. "But it's going to be very difficult," he told me, "because the owner is part of the Russian mafia, and he has the dolphins in his swimming pool."

O'Barry is involved in so many dolphin protests and rescues that it is hard to keep track of them. He has come to animals' aid in the Bahamas, Mexico, Nicaragua, Guatemala, Panama, Colombia, Haiti, Indonesia, Spain, Switzerland, Germany, Singapore, Britain, Egypt, Israel, China, Canada, and the Netherlands, among other places. "I never planned on being an activist," O'Barry said. "But one thing leads to another. Now, if there's a dolphin in trouble anywhere on this planet, my phone will ring."

We boarded the ferry and set off across the bay. Kii-Katsuura was a calmer town than Taiji, bigger and more sophisticated, and in the businesses and streets there was less anger directed at outsiders. Still, I noticed a lack of enthusiasm about our presence, store clerks suddenly becoming very busy when we approached, turning their backs or vanishing entirely.

O'Barry didn't take it personally. Actually, he told me, except for the dolphin hunt, he loved Japan and its people. As we walked along the street, he pointed out a bakery he visited each morning, and a toy shop that didn't bother to lock up at night: "There isn't even a door!" He nodded admiringly. In Japan, theft was almost nonexistent.

O'Barry stopped in front of a restaurant that displayed models of its menu items in the windows, molded out of plastic. "I usually pick what I want here," he said, pointing at the dishes. We went in and sat down at a table. When the waitress approached, O'Barry greeted her warmly in Japanese. After she took our orders I filled him in on our trip to the Whale Museum, an institution he fought with constantly. One time during an argument, the museum's manager, a man named Hiromitsu Nambu, had even waved a samurai sword at him. The two men were longtime enemies. Upset that the museum's dolphins suffered from blistering sunburn, O'Barry had offered to pay for an awning to shade the outdoor tanks. Nambu had agreed to let him. "That was six years ago, and he *still* hasn't done it," O'Barry said.

Sometimes when O'Barry talks about the cove, he just seems tired. Tired of fighting, tired of watching dolphins die, tired of the world's short attention span, tired of traveling here. But at other times, something interesting happens: his eyes become intense while his body stays relaxed, and all his energy flows into the moment. He isn't fearless—that would be silly—but he is ready, in a quiet way, to face anyone who would purposely hurt a dolphin. It was a strength that he'd developed over time, the way you'd build a muscle. In Taiji, the town was awful and the people could be horrid, but the cove's biggest challenge was a personal one: how do you survive your own sadness?

"What's it like when a bunch of dolphins are in there?" I asked. O'Barry looked down and rubbed his hands together. I noticed the dolphin tattoo near his left thumb, its edges faded by salt water and time. "It's heartbreaking," he said, from somewhere deep in his chest. "Because you *know* what's going to happen. I've seen as many as three hundred dolphins in there—pilot whales, false killer whales, bottlenose—all in one day! Yeah, when you're actually seeing it up close and personal it's much more . . . it's not like watching it in a movie. You can hear them, and at a certain angle you can sometimes see them throwing themselves onto the rocks, trying to escape." He paused again, struggling for words. "You know, it's . . . anguishing. 'Anguish' is the one where you can't do anything."

Facing heartbreak every day is not something most people want to do. Over the years, people have asked O'Barry why he chooses to devote his life to dolphins, putting them ahead of everything else, even his family. When you get to know him, however, you realize that he has no choice. O'Barry understands dolphins and what they represent: our entire relationship with nature. What happens in this corner of Japan matters to everyone. Domination, cruelty, making money by exploiting our fellow creatures: what a tragedy if we let those actions define us.

~~~~~~~

It was time to leave. I was tired of looking over my shoulder for yakuza, and the weather had turned so stormy that the dolphin-hunting boats had to stay at the docks. Maxwell was driving back to Osaka the next day, and I was going with her.

We had agreed to meet at four o'clock the next morning, rising in the dark so I could catch a noon flight from Osaka back to New York City. Outside my hotel window, the sky was black and rainy. Before I left, I texted O'Barry to say goodbye. I wished him good luck at the cove and asked if I could stay in touch. He replied immediately, which wasn't surprising; O'Barry rarely slept while he was here. He wasn't sure where he was headed after Taiji, he texted, but he would let me know. His travels might take him to the Philippines or back to Indonesia or hopefully to Denmark, where his wife and eight-year-old daughter, Mai Li, lived. He hadn't seen them in weeks. There was a marine park protest in Canada, and a baby dolphin who needed some help in Spain, and one particularly tough trip that he would need to make soon, to the Solomon Islands, a country he described as the most difficult place in the world for dolphins. In that country, dolphin teeth are used as money. If I didn't mind facing a level of hostility and danger that was even worse than in Taiji, I was welcome to join him. O'Barry wrote, "I still have a lot of unfinished work to do."

Chapter 6

A Sense of Self

It seems funny that in order to talk to the world's greatest expert on the dolphin brain, I had to go deep into the desert, far from the ocean. My destination was Kanab, Utah, a small town tucked into a dramatic landscape, near the North Rim of the Grand Canyon. The welcome sign at Kanab city limits lists the town's population as 4,410. That number had recently increased by one.

A few months earlier, neuroscientist Lori Marino, had packed up her lab at Emory University in Atlanta, said goodbye to her collection of dolphin brains, and moved here.

It wasn't Kanab itself that had drawn Marino, but one particular piece of it, Angel Canyon, where the Best

Friends Animal Sanctuary—one of the country's largest no-kill shelters—houses more than two thousand dogs, cats, horses, birds, rabbits, and other lucky creatures. This colorful community would be her new home. On Best Friends' 20,700-acre grounds, Marino's neighbors would include bunnies and eagles and piglets and donkeys and kittens. Which was exactly what she wanted. For Marino, the Best Friends Sanctuary was a kind of heaven, the perfect place to study the minds and emotions of animals.

As a neuroscientist, Marino specialized in brains: how they work, how they are built, how this fantastic gray matter between our ears directs our every perception. But instead of focusing her attention on humans, Marino had chosen instead to study dolphins. What was it about the dolphins' minds and social lives, she wondered, that had enabled them to live peaceably and successfully together for fifty-five million years? They had figured out a way to get along with one another, without destroying their environment—and these were things we humans still needed to learn ourselves.

Marino's work was well known in the scientific world: she had authored more than a hundred papers in her field. "The dolphin brain represents a different neurological scheme for intelligence," she said, explaining her research. "And it's a very complex intelligence." For one study she had collected 210 dolphin skulls from across the eons and run them through computer scanners to determine how their brains had evolved. Marino and her colleagues reconstructed 3-D models of dolphin brains from as far back as forty-seven million years ago, when they were relatively small and unspectacular, and charted them up to their current, turbo-charged state.

Curiously, as the dolphins' brains grew in size, their bodies shrank, their teeth became smaller, and they developed high-frequency hearing (their biological sonar). For us, that type of dramatic change didn't happen: as early human brains grew, during our own surge between eight hundred thousand and two hundred thousand years ago, our bodies and senses stayed more or less the same. We didn't suddenly turn into dwarves or sprout wings or learn to see through our noses. Our species has remained pretty consistent throughout our two million years of evolution, but the dolphins have shape-shifted in bold ways. On several occasions during their ninety-five-million-year existence they have morphed into entirely different creatures, adapting to life both on land and in the ocean. At various points in their evolution they have been huge solo predators with impressive fangs, chatty communicators packing powerful sonar, social networkers juggling complex relationships. Their bodies have gone through constant flux.

But what happened during the dolphins' history, Marino wondered, for their brains to undergo such a big growth spurt? It was an evolutionary puzzle. I wanted to talk to her about this, and other dolphin mysteries. She had looked into the animals' heads—literally.

Marino had also studied the more conceptual parts of the dolphin mind. In 2000, she and another scientist, Diana Reiss, conducted one of the most famous dolphin experiments of all time: a test to see if a bottlenose could recognize himself in a mirror. Most of the animals they'd tested couldn't. They ignored the mirror or were scared of it. The experiment worked like this: an animal—let's say a chimpanzee—was placed in front of a mirror and given a chance to examine it. Then the mirror was removed. Next, the scientists placed a bright-colored mark somewhere on the chimp's body—let's say they painted a bright pink stripe on his cheek. Then they brought back the mirror and showed him his reflection once again. If the chimp then leaned in to touch his mark and examine it in the mirror, he was said to have "passed" the test. He understood that the chimp with the odd pink stripe on his cheek was himself.

When Marino and Reiss first decided to try the mirror test with dolphins, only humans and our fellow great apes—chimpanzees, orangutans, and gorillas—had demonstrated self-awareness. So it was front-page science news when Marino and Reiss's two bottlenose dolphins, Presley and Tab, became the first non-primates to do this, mugging in front of the mirror, twisting their bodies around and flipping upside down to examine their marks. (Since then, elephants and magpies have also passed the mirror test.)

Though it might seem like no big deal, to conceive of your own identity is a brainy feat. The idea of a *self* is a pretty far-out abstraction, and to get that I am me and you are you and that we both have our own bodies and our own minds, but there's also a relationship between us— for a long time it was assumed that only people could do this. Self-awareness is not an ability that can be taken for granted. We don't begin to develop it until we're nearly two years old, along with feelings like sympathy and empathy. To know that dolphins are as conscious of their individuality as we are raises many important questions about their inner lives, and the ethics of how we treat them. What Reiss and Marino accomplished, really, was to prove that the dolphin in the tank is not a *what* but a *who*.

After succeeding with the mirror test, Marino did something unexpected: she vowed never to conduct research on captive dolphins again. Knowing how aware the dolphins were of their own situations, she could no longer justify keeping them in tanks, away from their pods and their natural lives. These days she refers to herself as a scientist-advocate, using everything she's learned about dolphins to argue for their well-being.

It isn't only dolphins Marino wants to stick up for. By moving to Angel Canyon she was signaling a new phase in her career, one in which she would use scientific facts to petition for all animals. And she isn't alone. Researchers around the globe are coming to the same conclusion—humans are not the only beings who matter—and new ideas are stirring about how the astonishing depth and breadth of other creatures makes it our moral responsibility to treat them with kindness and understanding. Now we have seen that elephants cry when they're sad, and some dogs can understand more words than toddlers, and sheep can pick faces out of a crowd. We've learned that chickens feel empathy and pigs express optimism. Scrub jays plan for the future. Pigeons are excellent at math. Thanks to YouTube, viral video clips of animals doing amazing stuff are a regular feature in our lives: cats rescuing their owners and rats cuddling stuffed toys and bonobos driving golf carts. But what will we do with this information?

In 2012, a group of scientists in Britain drafted "The Cambridge Declaration on Consciousness," which recognized the awesome abilities of nonhuman animals, down to the lowly earthworm (uses tools, makes decisions, decorates its home). "The body of scientific evidence is increasingly showing that most animals are conscious in the same way we are, and it's no longer something we can ignore," one journalist wrote of the proceedings.

Marino wanted to do more than agree with this declaration; she wanted to expand on it. Throughout her career she had watched fellow scientists perform all kinds of animal experiments, tinkering with their subjects in cruel ways and considering that standard practice. She wanted to do things differently, treating other creatures in the same way that we would like to be treated, respecting them as we would respect one another.

Kanab is a tiny town on the edge of a vast wilderness, with the Grand Canyon only a few hours up the road. It has a folksy feel. I was relieved to be out in fresh and appealing scenery, in a place where people were more interested in mountain biking than dolphin hunting. Back home in New York, I'd noticed that Taiji was stuck to me like tar. It made me unsettled, even nauseous sometimes. The nerve-racking noise of Manhattan—the pounding jackhammers and shrieking car alarms and endless traffic, the sirens, street cleaners, and clanging garbage trucks—seemed to rattle me more than ever. There were too many crowds and too much cement and not enough trees. I had trouble sleeping, and when I did, I had terrible dreams.

I couldn't get the dolphin hunt out of my head, especially since each day brought new bad news. Two days after I'd left, the hunters had captured a hundred pilot whales and killed every one of them, including mothers and calves, along with a pod of thirty bottlenose dolphins. Tim Burns, monitoring the cove, had written, "I had to recount numerous times to actually wrap my brain around such an alarming number. I'm speechless." The next day he reported: "Dolphins giving up a fight. Fishermen ramming them with boats and motors. Ruthless." Rumors circulated that the Taiji Fishermen's Union had run out of freezer space for dolphin meat and were now gathering dolphins for live export. A pod of ninety-two bottlenoses was captured next, and the selection process lasted for days—trainers from marine parks in Japan and China came to the cove and chose the dolphins they wanted. Most of the dolphins were sold, and the remainder—who were too old, too young, too scarred up, or too feisty—were butchered. Then a group of Risso's dolphins was driven into the cove. None of them made it back out.

Hitting the road has always seemed to me like a good way to deal with stress, so I had been itching to head out.

It was only after driving hours into the desert that I felt myself relaxing. There is no ocean in Kanab, but there is the peacefulness that arises when nature is bigger than you are. Five miles outside town, I spotted the Best Friends sign and turned into Angel Canyon.

Marino was waiting for me at the visitors' center, a neat brown building that melted into the landscape. She is petite, with shoulder-length sandy-brown hair and large, watchful hazel eyes. We sat outside on a deck, while beside us hummingbirds whirred around a feeder. Thunder rumbled in the distance. I told Marino that I was happy to be somewhere peaceful after being in Taiji. She nodded, looking pained. Marino hadn't been to the cove, but she'd seen plenty of video footage.

Marino was born and raised in Brooklyn, the oldest of two daughters in a traditional Italian family. She has a don't-mess-with-me New York accent and an expressive way of speaking. Her voice roams across octaves. From an early age, Marino knew that science was her path, though at first she didn't set out to study dolphins. The insects she found in her backyard, the family cat, her tank of guppies, the stars in the night sky—every creature, every question, every last bit of the natural world, *everything* enthralled her. Marino's childhood was filled with home telescopes, behavioral experiments with earthworms, wildly competitive science fairs: "the whole geek thing." Did life-forms exist on other planets? If yes, how would we talk to them? Did dogs dream? What was the mean size of a millipede? What was it like to be a bee? Her questions began.

As a graduate student, Marino first glimpsed the dolphin brain in books; at the Smithsonian Institution, while collecting data for her PhD dissertation, she encountered actual specimens. More than anything, she was struck by the brain's unusual appearance—it was oversize, rounder . . . *different.* While everyone else in her field studied the brains of chimpanzees and other apes, the animals most like ourselves, Marino was drawn to the weird, unfamiliar, and far more ancient architecture of the dolphin brain. "We're primates—I get it," she said, with a shrug. "But there is more than one way to be smart."

Marino and her colleagues had some powerful tools at their fingertips, including computer imaging that helped them explore the deepest unknown territories of the dolphin brain. Now they could create a 3-D model of a brain, rotate it, zoom in on it, and measure every part of its structure in precise detail. As their understanding of the dolphin brain grew, they discovered that it is every bit as extraordinary as our own. "There's folklore about dolphin brains that says they're big but kind of simple," Marino said, shaking her head. "That's old stuff. We know now that it is a very complicated brain with a very wide range of types of cells. Their wiring's different. But it is just as complex—it could be *more* complex."

One of the most striking things about the dolphin brain is that its neocortex—the most recently evolved part of the brain that enables us to do sophisticated stuff like reason, use our senses, socialize with others, consciously think—is constructed in an utterly original way. It's an impressive structure: in humans, this area occupies 80 percent of our brain's volume. "There's a basic plan for the neocortex," Marino explained. "In all mammals it's layered." Ours is made up of six layers, and each layer contains specific cells that interpret certain types of information. But dolphins and whales have only five layers. "They're missing Layer 4," she said. "And the reason that's such a big deal is because, in primates, Layer 4 is where all the input for the lower parts of the brain come into the neocortex and get integrated." She raised her eyebrows. "So if they don't have a Layer 4, where's the information coming in?" There were some theories, she added, but no one really knew the answer. "The way information enters their brain, gets tossed around, and out of their brain—it's *completely* different."

If you pulled a neocortex out of a human or dolphin head, Marino told me, you could unfold it like a sheet. Ours is thicker, but theirs covers more area. The dolphin neocortex has more crimps and wrinkles, more surface area for action to happen. In their brains, the region that deals with hearing is located at the top of their heads, while our hearing is processed in the temporal lobe, at the bottom back of our heads. Dolphins have also rearranged the way they integrate sound and visual input; their processing areas are located right next to each other, resulting in lightning quick responses. "This is a brain that is built for speed," Marino said. "The rate at which they process information is *astounding*. Everything's faster!" She smiled, her eyes wide. "I mean, *are you kidding me?* We can't even imagine."

One type of brain cells neuroscientists find fascinating are spindle cells, also called von Economo neurons (VENs). Humans and dolphins both have these cells in their brains, in the areas responsible for high-level abilities like judgment, intuition, and awareness—and so do whales, elephants, great apes, and macaque monkeys—but in the animal kingdom, VENs are unusual. Even their appearance is exotic: while many neurons look like wonky starbursts, their dendrite arms reaching across synapses to send and receive signals from nearby cells, VENs shoot out like bolts of forked lightning. They are also about four times bigger than most other brain cells. "They're like superstar neurons," Marino said. "And we see them in very interesting parts of the brain."

Recently, researchers discovered that when the VENs

in a person's brain are damaged, dementia and antisocial behavior can result. Losing these cells can cause us to forget what we're supposed to do and say. We seem to need our VENs to get along with one another, to know if we've made a mistake, to control our emotions. VENs appear to play a role in our ability to trust, to joke around, even to love one another. Scientists still don't understand the exact role these superstar neurons play in the brain, but they do know that dolphins and whales have about three times more of them than we do.

One of the main reasons any creature would need a big, elaborate brain in the first place, scientists believe, is to deal with the details of a thriving social life. Keeping track of family and friends and acquaintances in a large community, figuring out things like who owes you a favor, and who once betrayed the group, and who treated your grandma with special kindness but is also related to the guy who stole your brother's girlfriend—the fine web of interactions between hundreds of individuals—is as challenging for dolphins as it is for us. We need every bit of our brainpower to navigate these relationships, using everything from memory to reasoning to communication skills.

So dolphins developed such big brains to keep track of their social lives? Yes, probably, Marino said, but it's not quite that simple. "When you say 'social,' well, you have

Rough-toothed dolphins,
fin to fin.

A bottlenose dolphin
hunts for a snack on
the reef.

A spinner dolphin near
the Big Island, Hawaii.

Fungie, the famous bottlenose dolphin who has lived in the
waters near Dingle, Ireland, for more than thirty years.

A pilot whale named Moby lived
a brief, unhappy life at
Marine Studios, Florida, in 1948.

A Risso's dolphin spyhops, sticking his head
out of the water to look around. As he gets
older, his skin will turn even more silvery.

Spinner dolphins near the Big Island, Hawaii.

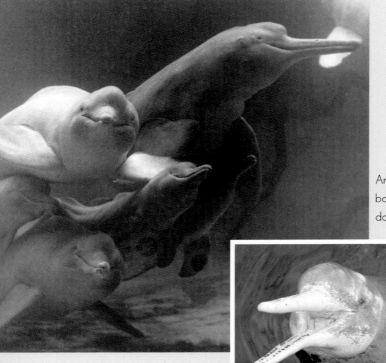

Amazon River botos, or pink dolphins.

A melon-head pod in the waters around Hawaii.

Orcas, also known as killer whales, are the largest species of dolphin.

A false killer whale in motion.

Above: Dolphins captured in Taiji, Japan. *Below:* Each year, thousands of dolphins are killed in Taiji's notorious cove. Many other dolphins are taken from their families and sold to marine parks around the world.

Above: One of the earliest dolp[hin]
artworks we know of, from th[e]
Minoan civilization.

Left: Thera, now known as
Santorini, is a place full of
mystery—and dolphins.

Below: The lost city of Akrotir[i]
a site that has yielded many
dolphin artworks, and clues to [the]
Minoans, a people who had a m[uch]
closer relationship with nature
than we do now.

Above: Minoan dolphin fresco in the Palace of Knossos, Greece.
Below: Minoan marine-style artworks found in the ashes of Thera.

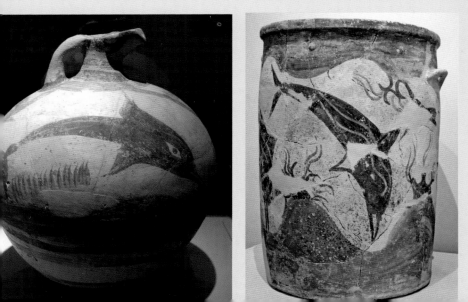

The author swimming with a pod of spinner dolphins in Kona, Hawaii.

Spotted dolphins,
curious as usual.

to have good communication to have a social culture," she said. "You have to have this; you have to have that. So it all gets wound together. But it's probably the best story we have right now." Doesn't it make sense, I asked, that when dolphins became smaller and less ferocious, when their teeth shrank and their brains grew, that they would begin to rely more on the group for survival? "They would need each other," Marino agreed.

In fact, dolphins are so tightly bound to others in their pods that they may be far more interconnected than we are. "When you look at their brain you can definitely see how this could be an animal that takes sociality to another level," Marino said. She pointed out that scientists can't explain why an entire pod of dolphins or whales might strand themselves on the beach when only one or two individuals are sick, or why, when they're herded into the Taiji cove, they huddle together and don't jump the nets to escape. To us, it would be logical to save ourselves if we could. But what if, for dolphins, *the entire group* was part of the self?

The possibility that a dolphin may think of the other dolphins around him as part of himself is an incredible idea. While we think of our *self* as stopping at the edge of our body, completely separate from others, a dolphin's sense of self might be quite different. A dolphin's awareness, his concerns, even his survival instincts might extend out into the world around him. And if a dolphin's *self* had this flexible boundary, he would relate to others in his pod in a kind of shared existence that we can't even imagine.

"There is some sort of cohesiveness in them that I don't think we get quite yet, but it accounts for a lot of the behavior that seems strange to us," Marino said. She took a sip of her tea and leaned over to pet a dog that had wandered up to our table. In a field behind us, two horses cantered across the grass, whinnying and shaking their manes. "I think a lot of it comes down to emotional attachment," she continued. "And I think there is a very strong sense in them that if something happens to the group, it happens to *you*."

Marino pointed out that one particular area of the dolphin's brain, known as the limbic system, might well have adapted for this type of intense interconnectedness. It is an ancient part of the brain: the seat of emotions, memory, and smell. While most vertebrates evolved this region early and kept it pretty much intact, once again the dolphins came up with their own design. Since there are no odors underwater, their hippocampus, a region linked to their sense of smell, is small. But another part of their limbic system, called the paralimbic area, grew large and so densely jammed with neurons that it burped out an extra lobe. There's a huge amount of tissue packed into this area, and scientists think it relates to *feeling*. No other mammal has anything quite like it. "It suggests that these animals are doing something very sophisticated or complex while they're processing emotions," Marino said.

That's the thing about brains. You can guess what they're up to, but right now, anyway, we really don't know for sure. The human brain contains hundreds of billions of cells busily engaged in thousands of trillions of unknown, vital tasks. "There is no neuroscientist on the planet that can claim he or she knows how we go from this gray matter to being conscious," Marino said. "*Nobody* knows. It is a complete mystery."

Yet we're not entirely clueless. Our ability to study the brain's anatomy has given us information, hints, and ideas about what's going on in there. We can examine how dolphin or human brains are constructed, and then compare that to behavior. We can assume that a large brain size relative to body size makes for a more intelligent creature, although what *intelligent* means, exactly, is hard to define. We can't deny that tiny-brained animals like crows or octopuses are capable of very clever feats, while humans, with our big brains, engage in all kinds of self-destructive nonsense. Trying to rank dolphin intelligence against human intelligence is like comparing submarines to airplanes, or the color pink to the color purple. They can't write things down; we don't have sonar. Rating animals' brainpower is a difficult task.

That doesn't matter, Marino said. We need to try. What we have to do, she believes, is carefully observe the facts for each species and keep our emotions off to the side. "In other words: dolphins recognize themselves in mirrors. Does this mean they are more brilliant than dogs, who do not? I don't know," she said. "I just know this is a capacity they have that many other animals don't have. And it means something."

The day had grown hotter as we talked so we moved to a shaded patio overlooking a rugged canyon. A vegetarian lunch buffet had been laid out, so Marino and I stopped to get salads. Staff members emerged from their offices, along with several dogs who were keeping them company while they worked. A group of high-school volunteers wearing Best Friends T-shirts came in, too. "The person who has probably done the most to help us understand dolphin intelligence is Lou Herman," Marino said, after we sat down with our plates. "His work was *superb*."

Louis Herman was a psychology professor emeritus at the University of Hawaii. His studies on dolphin perception, memory, and communication were groundbreaking, jaw-dropping—any admiring adjective you'd care to insert. With scientific rigor and a lot of creativity, Herman showed just how smart dolphins can be. "My thought was, 'Okay, so you have this pretty brain. Let's see what you can do with it,'" he told *National Geographic*.

Herman's research was based in Honolulu, at the Kewalo Basin Marine Mammal Laboratory. From 1970 to 2004, he worked with bottlenose dolphins, teaching them a sign language and another language based on sounds, and then testing how well they grasped various concepts— including many tricky abstract notions that animals are really not supposed to be able to understand.

But Herman's bottlenoses surprised everyone. They responded to complicated sentences and knew exactly how the word order, or syntax, changed their meanings. They got instantly that a command like "take the surfboard to the Frisbee" was different than "take the Frisbee to the surfboard," and they adjusted their movements accordingly. Even when the instructions were brand-new, tasks they'd never been given before, the dolphins responded quickly and correctly. When they were asked to do something impossible, like bring the tank window to the surfboard, they wouldn't attempt any action. They just stared at their trainers, as if to say, "*Come on.* You and I both know that can't be done."

Herman's dolphins could distinguish left from right, even when the directions were suddenly reversed. They understood the concepts of presence and absence. Using their flippers to press paddles that indicated yes or no, the dolphins responded correctly when asked if a person or object—a boy, another dolphin, a ball, a box—was in their tank or not. They could listen to a series of eight sounds and then indicate whether a ninth sound had been previously played. They grasped the ideas of "same" or "different," and "less" or "more." They reported whether they were "sure" or "unsure" of an answer to a difficult question. When asked to perform "new" behaviors they immediately began to innovate, synchronizing their movements perfectly.

Herman also proved that dolphins understand what we mean when we're pointing; that they can identify their own body parts; that they realize television is a representation of reality. They can remember objects, locations, and instructions even over time, recalling information as necessary. They are masterful mimics, able to imitate sounds and movements with ease. With no prior instruction, when a trainer lifted a leg in the air and asked the dolphin to do the same, the dolphin lifted his tail.

Not only were the dolphins capable of understanding everything Herman asked of them (and probably far more), they picked everything up at warp speed. "When you work with them, they're always one step ahead," Marino said. "They get things much quicker. They do things much faster." She laughed. "I mean, you can tell they're impatient because they have to deal with slow humans."

The day before I flew back to New York I drove back to Las Vegas, and stayed there overnight. My own brain was spinning after talking to Marino about the dolphins' brains. There were so many questions I still wanted to ask; I felt as though I could have stayed at Best Friends for months. I would have happily volunteered to clean out the pig pens or the horse stables if it meant the chance to find out more about the inner lives of the sanctuary's animals.

Sleep came quickly that night, but strangely. In my dreams I found myself adrift in a stormy ocean in the moonlit dark, wind howling and waves battering rocks, while all around me the dorsal fins of dolphins rose and fell, coming dangerously close to shore. To avoid the pounding surf I dove, and I could see perfectly underwater, as though I were wearing goggles. Below the surface, the dolphins were trying to get my attention. They were excited, gathered around a doorway under the ocean. The door was bright turquoise and quite small, as though built for hobbits (or dolphins). They pushed their beaks against it and nudged me forward. I opened the door and swam through. On the other side, the water was darker, the color draining from marine blue to inky navy to a blackness that felt absolutely still. Then I realized I wasn't in water in any longer, but space. The medium was rich, as thick as oil, filled with grandeur and overwhelming mystery. I swam deeper and deeper, beyond anything I could recognize but the fast sweep of dolphins moving around me in the beautiful, terrible void, my own heartbeat, and the winking of a million stars.

Chapter 7

High Frequency

~~~~~~~~

I was in Los Angeles when Joan Ocean emailed, inviting me back to Hawaii. If I could come to Kona the following week, she wrote, I could be her guest at a five-day workshop she was hosting called "Dolphins, Teleportation, and Time Travel." In the mornings, we would swim with wild dolphins along the coast. In the evenings, we would talk about dolphins. "The dolphins have been amazing lately," she told me. "I don't like to always use that word, but it definitely applies here."

I packed enthusiastically. I was curious about why the words "teleportation," "time travel," and "dolphins" were being used in the same sentence. Spending five days with Ocean in Dolphinville would be a full immersion, and I knew that I'd be surrounded by people with colorful—some would say crazy—beliefs. Many of her followers believe that dolphins are visitors from faraway stars, wise elders who've beamed themselves down to Earth to teach us vital lessons—ideas that seem to come straight from science fiction. Ocean's workshop would be the opposite of a scientific gathering. It was a place for dolphin lovers with wild imaginations to get together. Which seemed like a great reason to go.

Dolphins are a riddle—among the many mysteries in our lives. We only figured out a few centuries ago that the Earth revolved around the sun; as recently as 1850, no one knew that germs cause disease. Even now, in a time when we've landed rovers on Mars, the ocean on our blue planet is largely unknown to us, and so are the creatures who live beneath its surface. Often, I found myself wondering: What *don't* we know about dolphins? For that matter, what don't we know about ourselves? What don't we know about everything? The answer to all of the above is: plenty.

You might be surprised, for instance, to learn that rather than the five senses you think you have—plus a "sixth sense" if you count intuition—humans have at least twenty-one means of perception. Our biological toolkit includes proprioception (the position of your body in space), chronoception (a sense of the passage of time), nociception (the awareness of pain), and thermoception (a sense of hot and cold), among others. There are sensors throughout our bodies—in our brains, blood, skin, hearts, cells—registering even the subtlest cues. One recently discovered sense is magnetoreception, or the ability to track the planet's magnetic fields—and dolphins definitely have it. Sharks, birds, sea turtles, bats, butterflies, and honeybees also use it to navigate. No one knows exactly how it works, but scientists think that magnetite crystals in the creatures' heads subtly pull them in one direction or another, guiding them across great distances with precision.

In other superpower news, people and monkeys have managed to move objects using only their thoughts. Dolphins emit sonar through their foreheads. Birds can feel earthquakes coming hours in advance. Prayer has healed people. Brain surgery patients placed into temporary comas were able to recall—in remarkable detail—conversations that occurred in the operating room while they were technically dead. So what other unusual senses and abilities might humans—or dolphins—have that we don't even realize?

It's easy to dismiss what you don't understand. It's unsettling to think that the world might be weirder than advertised. Daily, we forget how miraculous everything is, down to the tiniest subatomic speck. According to quantum physics, what we see through our eyes and process through our senses is just one interpretation of reality. If you were to swap brains with a dolphin, your reality would change, too. And these are findings that we *have* proven. Why should anything surprise us?

~~~~~

"I know many of you have been here before and have heard the basic dolphin information," Ocean said, looking out at the packed room, people in chairs, on the floor, anywhere they could find a seat. "So tonight I thought I'd talk about the far-out stuff." She smiled; the crowd whooped. "We can take it, Joan!" a man wearing a Sasquatch T-shirt shouted. "We're ready!" a woman with a purple streak in her hair yelled.

It was Day 3 of the workshop and I had just arrived, pulling into the driveway at Ocean's home, Sky Island Ranch, as the evening's program began. I wedged myself into the room and looked around. There were at least seventy people here, slightly more women than men, a wide span of ages and nationalities. There were Australians, Brits, and Germans. A South African and a New Zealander. Several Canadians. A handful of kids under ten.

Ocean leaned back in her chair, a white swivel lounger.

"There is a longing in people to have contact with dolphins," she began. "It's not some whim. We have a deep soul connection."

Her own dolphin experiences began in 1978, at a workshop where the group leader had played tapes of dolphin clicks and whistles, day and night, at top volume. "So maybe that's where everything started," Ocean mused. "Maybe they were saying things and I was picking it up." Over the past thirty-five years, she had swum with twenty-eight species of whales and dolphins in twenty countries. "We are here to teach you to move beyond the limits of the five senses," Ocean felt the animals tell her as she swam among them. "We encourage you to communicate with us in the unexplored domains of the sixth sense and beyond." Plus, the dolphins added, it was possible to merge the senses together: "You will begin to smell images, hear feelings, and see sounds."

Though such a mix-up of senses might sound absurd, it actually happens: scientists call it synesthesia. People with this neurological condition—and there are quite a few of them—experience such unusual things as feeling colors, tasting shapes, smelling emotions, and seeing numbers as objects. It's especially common in the creative fields: many famous writers and artists have had synesthesia. The inventor Nikola Tesla was said to possess it; musician Pharrell

Williams has it, too. In fact, research has suggested that we are all born with these abilities, but most of us lose them fairly quickly.

Ocean continued with her story. "I was swimming with the dolphins for about two months before they included me in their pod," she told us. "The pod field of energy can be very wide. Remember, they can communicate over long distances to each other, so they don't need to be side by side like we do." As Ocean swam among the dolphins in a relaxed state, she would mentally ask them questions and then wait for images to pop into her mind, which she took as answers. One unexpected thing the dolphins told her was that she should pay more attention to opera.

Ocean bought some opera recordings and listened to them, trying to hit the high notes herself. Compared to dolphins, however, we have a very limited range. They can hear extremely high-pitched, or high-frequency, sounds, up to eight times higher than we can. (Dolphins, whales, and porpoises have the most impressive hearing ranges of any creatures in the world.) Ocean believes the dolphins' ability to hear and make sounds at very high frequencies— also called ultrasound—is not just a means for them to navigate and hunt fish, but an advanced form of communication that can alter reality. "These tones can transform all things," she has written. "They can heal and change our bodies and our environments."

Even if you don't share Ocean's New Age beliefs, you're probably aware that everything around us is vibrating at all times, even the heaviest solid objects, and that energy waves can have great force, even if we can't see them or hear them (think of earthquakes, lasers, microwave ovens). At extremely high frequencies—far higher than dolphins can generate—ultrasound has been used to destroy tumor cells, heal broken bones, and stop wounds from bleeding. It can even cause matter to levitate: drops of alcohol, plastic beads, and matches have all been lifted off the ground by sound. Blasts of high-frequency sound *can,* as Ocean claims, change the physical property of a substance. Liquid can turn to jelly. Bacteria can disintegrate. Water can be zapped into mist.

Even in the range that we can hear, sound has powerful effects. In a study done at a London hospital, researchers found that patients healed faster when soothing music was played in their rooms. Also, the hospital staff was happier, babies thrived, everyone's blood pressure was lowered, and surgeons performed better. On the flip side, sound can also be used as a weapon: strong low-frequency sound waves can interfere with people's respiratory tracts, making it hard for them to breathe.

Given all this, it seems logical to wonder if the dolphins' sonar might have some healing properties, and if swimming with them might help cure illnesses—but scientists have not found any evidence of this. Ocean had her own theory. "It's not that dolphins heal people," she told the group. "It's that being with them helps people regain their natural healthy state." She urged us to ask the spinners for help if we needed it. But the request had to be made from the heart, she stressed. "What carries the communication are your feelings of love. Feelings of caring. And you know that feeling when it comes over you." Her voice cracked with emotion. "When you're feeling that love in your heart—*that's* when you're communicating."

~~~~~~

At dawn the next morning I drove to the harbor to meet up with everyone, and the boats that would take us out to the dolphins. At the docks, we split into two groups. Most people boarded a large, double-decker boat, but Ocean waved me onto a powerboat that only took eight. While the bigger boat loaded its heap of gear, our captain, a Santa-Claus-shaped man named Kit, suggested that we leave immediately, because he'd heard on the radio that a pod of pilot whales was cruising by a few miles offshore.

Without waiting for the other boat, we headed out. Searching for a pod of pilot whales on the move is like looking for a needle in a giant haystack, but Kit seemed confident. Somehow, I knew we would find them. I was thinking about what other fantastic creatures we might find so far offshore and watching the water turn a deeper and deeper blue as we sped away from land, when the radio squawked again: another sighting, closer. We drove about a mile and stopped, rocking on a light swell. Everything was quiet, the water lapping against the hull.

"Whooooofff!" A pilot whale surfaced with a sudden gust of air, a hundred yards away from us. "Poooooshhh!" Another whale came up right beside him. Their black backs rolled and dove; we could see their round heads, their swept-back dorsal fins and thick bodies. Then, more fins, all around. These dolphins were three times bigger than the average spinner. "There are at least forty in the pod," Ocean counted. "And they have some calves with them."

Kit drove ahead. He would position us far in front of the whales so we could jump in and swim with them as they passed. I fiddled with my mask, feeling nervous. I'd never been frightened around dolphins, but at twenty-feet long and weighing three tons, these were more like orcas. Also, I was aware of pilot whales' reputation as stubborn, sometimes cranky animals. I thought back to one scary incident that had occurred in these waters, when a pilot whale snatched a swimmer by the ankle and yanked her down forty feet below the surface. The woman barely escaped drowning.

Still, I knew I would take the risk to observe them

underwater. Compared to the spinners, the pilots are an exotic tribe. These were short-finned pilot whales, but there are also long-finned pilot whales, the two species closely resembling one another. Both are members—along with false killer whales, pygmy killer whales, melon-headed whales, and orcas—of the group of dolphins known as blackfish. Like orcas, pilot whale pods are focused around matriarchs, mammoth mommas who run the show, and whose sons stay with them throughout their lives. Grandmothers, too, play a central role: for up to fifteen years after their breeding years are over (at around age thirty-five), female pilot whales continue to help nurse and babysit their podmates' calves, boosting their survival chances.

Kit cut the engines and told us we could slip in quietly, two by two. The ocean was crystal clear. Even with such perfect visibility I couldn't see the seafloor out here: we were floating in water three miles deep. "Starboard!" Kit shouted, pointing. I saw a pair of whales surface nearby, headed straight for us. I dove and so did the pilots, and soon they loomed into view beneath me, two huge adults with a calf tucked below them, swimming by slowly and sounding me with their sonar clicks. Sunbeams shone through the water and danced across their bodies like spotlights.

The whales disappeared into the blue and we climbed back on the boat; Kit shuttled us ahead and then dropped us in their path again. If the pilot whales didn't want us around them they could have simply dove out of sight: they can go fifteen minutes between breaths. One of their hunting strategies for squid, their main prey, is to dive as fast as they can, twenty miles per hour, down to three thousand feet (almost two-thirds of a mile), an effort so strenuous they've been nicknamed "the cheetahs of the deep sea." Pilot whales are even thought to compete with sperm whales for their favorite meal: *Architeuthis,* the giant squid. At times, they have been spotted swimming along with four-foot-long tentacles trailing out of their mouths.

The pilots didn't shy away from us. They passed closer this time, allowing the calf to come closer. The tiny whale was curious, eyeing us. I hovered, lost in awe. Time stretched like taffy. At one point I realized that I'd forgotten to breathe. My lungs tightened but I felt no panic, even though I was twenty feet down. If more people swam with dolphins and whales in the ocean, I thought as I kicked to the surface, we would all be so much happier.

While we were in the water, Kit heard radio reports of a spinner superpod just up the coast, a gathering of three to four hundred dolphins. We decided to head over there and see if we could find them. As we drove, I told Ocean how blissful I'd felt among the pilot whales, unconcerned with ordinary things like gravity and time and even air.

She nodded, laughing. "My whole goal is to get people into that place," she said. "It's love and gratitude. And it means a lot."

The spinners were easy to find. There were so many of them that even from a distance they were visible, leaping one after another, whirling through the air like rockets and splashing down dramatically. When we drew closer to the pod, which stretched as far as we could see, the dolphins shot to the front of the boat, jockeying to surf our bow waves. They came speeding in from all directions, and when we slowed, they slowed along with us, circling the boat. We drifted above a coral reef teeming with jewel-colored fish, and if the dolphins were hoping we would join them, they couldn't have chosen a better spot. For hours we swam there, and so did they. For hours, we played.

≈≈≈

If the New Age world has proclaimed dolphins to be magical creatures whose presence enchants us, it should be acknowledged that other, older groups arrived at this conclusion first. At least fifteen thousand years ago California's earliest inhabitants, the Native Americans of the Chumash nation, referred to themselves as the Dolphin People. Their history spelled it out. This tribe was not merely friendly to dolphins, they considered the dolphins to be their direct relatives. The Pacific Ocean was not just the magnificent vista they gazed at from their villages; it was their ancestral home. The Chumash were hunters and gatherers, known for their weaving and bead-making skills, their expertise in paddling their agile redwood-planked canoes, and their peaceful, resourceful ways.

More than twenty thousand Chumash people once lived in fire-lit settlements along the central and southern California coast, as well as on the nearby Channel Islands: Santa Cruz, Santa Rosa, Anacapa, and San Miguel. Then the Spanish arrived in the eighteenth century, bringing conquest and disease: by 1900 only two hundred Chumash were left. But despite this tragedy, the tribe's past has not been forgotten. Its heritage remains, and so does its bond with dolphins.

At Malibu's northern edge, in fact, next door to a row of multimillion-dollar houses, there is a replica of a real Chumash village. Its name is Wishtoyo (the Chumash word for "rainbow"), and its cofounder, a Chumash man named Mati Waiya, built it so he could reintroduce his culture's traditions to the world.

I drove down the dirt road to the village on a late-summer afternoon, the dust from my tires billowing red and gold in the dusky light. If you weren't looking for

Wishtoyo, you would never find it—it isn't a showy place. Tucked on a cliff above the Pacific, its buildings blend into the landscape so well it's as though they've sprung from the earth itself, and actually, they have. Wishtoyo's six dome-shaped dwellings are made of willow branches and woven reeds, their entrances draped with deerskin and framed by whalebones and antlers, stones and seashells. Their floors are soft sand.

As I pulled in to park, three huge German shepherds came loping toward me, followed by Waiya himself, a tall and hearty man in his fifties. His waist-length black hair was pulled back and secured by two long slivers of bone. A smaller bone pierced his nose, and he had a sleek mustache and beard that looked like they were tattooed onto his skin. Waiya wore strands of beaded necklaces, a tribal print sarong, and a sleeveless T-shirt that revealed thickly muscled arms. He was barefoot. A raptor claw hung from his left ear.

Waiya greeted me, and we began to talk about dolphins. "We're a maritime people," he told me, as we walked through the village. "The dolphins are our relatives, our brothers and sisters." The Chumash, he explained, had names for everything around them. "*A'lul'koy* is our blue dolphin. Malibu is called *Humaliwu*, where the waves crash loudly. *Muwu* is the big ocean." He stopped in front of a building that was about the size and shape of an igloo. "It's called an *ap*," Waiya said. "A family would sleep in here." We ducked inside, followed by Sumo, one of the German shepherds. The air was cooler under the dome, and it smelled of sage. Waiya picked up two long condor feathers, which he waved in the air as he spoke.

"The creation story is really what a lot of it is about," he said. "Our people came here from Limuw—Santa Cruz Island." Hutash, the Earth Goddess, had called the Chumash from the island to the mainland, Waiya explained. She promised them a paradise for future generations, and she made a bridge out of a rainbow. Then she told them to walk across it, over the ocean. But she warned them not to look down. "Well, some of the people couldn't resist and they did look down," Waiya continued, "and they got dizzy and fell. As they hit the water and started to sink, Hutash asked our God, Kakunupmawa, our creator, our grandfather, 'Don't let them die.' Down they went and as they fell to the bottom of the ocean, their bodies started becoming silky and then these fins came out, and they surfaced and took their first breath of air. They turned into *A'lul'koy*. The people became dolphins."

One of the most important Chumash ceremonies was called the Dolphin Dance. Now, as an elder himself, Waiya performed it. He showed me a photo of the dance in progress. In the picture, Waiya was wearing a dolphin dancer costume, and his body was painted with black and white stripes and dots. He also wore an elaborate feather headdress and a skirt. In both hands he was shaking *wansaks*, clapper sticks that make a noise like dolphins. Fire blazed in front of him. "It's a trippy dance," he said, grinning.

At Wishtoyo Waiya hosted groups of all ages, teaching his people's traditions, celebrating the seasons, and holding retreats. One of his main audiences was elementary school classes. "I can put fifty kids in here," Waiya said, waving his arm around the *ap*. "I have a PowerPoint presentation about marine life. I'll tell them all about the ocean, about ecosystems and endangered species, all these different ways of looking at the environment and balance and understanding, not just the science and the laws, but how it's a part of you and you're a part of it."

Once he got rolling, Waiya's voice rose and fell with the rhythm of a chant. It was easy to envision a bunch of kids sitting in here, having the time of their lives. "I tell them, 'If you love that ocean, that whale, that dolphin, that forest, that river, that bear, those eagles—all those beautiful things that are part of the world,'" Waiya said, "'then you've got it. It's already in you.'"

Currently, Waiya is working to create a network of

protected areas along the California coast, patches of ocean that will be fully restored and allowed to flourish as they did thousands of years ago. "We gotta do the right thing somewhere," Waiya said, as we left the *ap* and walked to the edge of the bluff. "Our oceans are the bloodline of our world."

The sun was sinking down over the Pacific, while the moon rose above it like a pale shadow. Behind us, traffic streamed along Highway One, but all I could hear was the sound of the waves. Below us, silhouetted in the amber light, two surfers waited for the day's last sets, floating among soft rafts of kelp. I wished I were out there with them, that I could take off my shoes and stay here longer, while my emails and to-do lists stayed somewhere else, at least for a little while.

I mentioned this to Waiya, and he ran with it. "We're living in a computer screen!" he said. "All this technology is gonna be our demise. And these health ailments that we're getting, diabetes and obesity, and now our social skills are being threatened because we're texting and we're emailing and we're not even talking anymore." He inhaled deeply, sweeping his condor feathers across Wishtoyo, as though blessing it.

In the Chumash tradition, the dolphins have a special significance because they live under water, but also breathe air: they exist in more than one realm. "The *A'lul'koy* represents the west," Waiya said, nodding at the horizon, "where the day ends and your dreams begin, where the land and the ocean meet. It's transition, where our people exit this world for the spirit world. And one day will be our last sunset and we, too, will transition from this life to the next." As if to illustrate his point, the moon suddenly grew brighter, taking its place on the stage.

"There's another dimension out there," I said, pointing to the ocean.

"Oh yeah," Waiya said, bowing his head. "It's real."

Chapter 8

The Most Amazing Animals on the Planet

~~~~~~

*O*nly two miles off the Kona coast, the ocean plunges a mile deep in a long, steep slope to the seafloor. There are only a few places in the world where you can be standing on shore drinking your morning coffee and in less than thirty minutes find yourself suspended over the abyss— Kona is one of them. Which is why Robin Baird, a biologist who studies deepwater dolphin species, spends so much of his time there.

While the spinner dolphins hunt in the depths at night and then return to the shallows during the day, other dolphin species hardly ever approach the shore. As a result, we know very little about them. About six weeks a year, Baird and his team cruise the deep waters off Hawaii in their research boat, searching for these uncommon dolphins—false killer whales, pygmy killer whales, melon-headed whales, rough-toothed dolphins, Risso's dolphins, and striped dolphins—along with their more familiar cousins: pilot whales, bottlenoses, spinners, and spotted dolphins. Every once in a while, they'll come across orcas passing by. Baird also encounters the dolphins' close relatives, beaked whales and sperm whales, and he gathers information about them, too. In all, he studies eighteen types of toothed whales around Hawaii.

I wanted to learn more about the deepwater dolphins, and Baird was the guy to ask. "I've always been interested in rare species," he told me, describing how he grew up on British Columbia's Vancouver Island, a place full of natural wonder. As a young boy Baird was exposed to orcas, not just the captives who had lived at his local aquarium, Sealand of the Pacific, but the magnificent Northwest pods that swam along the coastline near his home.

Later, when he grew older and became a marine scientist, Baird studied the orcas' hunting methods, strategies that require them to communicate precisely, cooperate extensively, and work to achieve a shared goal. Any long-lived species that can do these things, he said, should be counted among the smartest on earth. Knowing how impressive the orcas are, Baird was doubly fascinated when he saw his first false killer whale, or pseudorca, an even more mysterious ocean citizen. False killer whales are about two-thirds the size of orcas, with similar thick, cone-shaped teeth, a more tapered physique, and dark, muscular bodies. These dolphins are often described as fast, agile, volatile, emotional—and extremely clever.

This wasn't just Baird's first glimpse of a false killer whale: it was the first sighting reported in Canada, ever. The animal was stranded on shore and didn't survive, but finding only one body was a relief. These dolphins form such close bonds with one another that they often strand in large numbers. Once, more than eight hundred false killer whales died on a beach in Argentina; groups of more than a hundred have stranded in South Africa, Europe, Australia, New Zealand, and Florida, among other places. Baird's interest was stoked. He and his colleagues studied the body, extracting every bit of information they could from it.

The scientists found that the dead whale's liver was overloaded with mercury and DDT, extremely high levels of poisonous toxins. In the twenty-eight years since then, Baird has collected tissue samples from forty other false killer whales and discovered a disturbing pattern: they're *all* highly contaminated. Their bodies are saturated with PCBs, dioxins, flame retardants, heavy metals, pesticides—

some of the worst cancer-causing chemicals known. Many of these long-lived toxins, known as persistent organic pollutants (POPs), have been outlawed for decades, but they still linger in the environment. "Over time they've been incorporated into food webs and dispersed across ocean basins," Baird says. "You can't see these chemicals and they're not killing animals outright; they're just making them more susceptible to infections and if they get an infection they'll have greater difficulty dealing with it." Recently, Baird had lead the effort to get false killer whales added to the endangered species list, using his research to show that their numbers are fast declining.

False killer whales also suffer from a problem that plagues dolphins all over the world, from tiny Hector's dolphins right up to orcas: as top predators, their diet consists of the same fish we like to eat, and in recent decades we have vacuumed the oceans, wiping out one fish population after the next with our destructive methods. Overfishing, bottom trawling, taking fish before they're old enough to reproduce, netting and long-lining practices that kill everything in their path—these shortsighted practices have landed both humans and dolphins in a pinch: we're running out of seafood.

Though dolphins have been hunting in the planet's waters for eons longer than we have, they're no match for the high-tech fishing industry. In offshore waters, industrial fleets the size of cities scour the seas with radar, sonar, and spotter aircraft, scooping up everything that swims. Around Hawaii, most of the false killer whales Baird encounters have visible injuries from run-ins with fisheries. Their dorsal fins are lacerated and deformed, sometimes all but razored off, from getting entangled in longlines. Recently, Baird told me, a false killer whale had washed up dead on the Big Island with five fishhooks in its stomach.

〰〰〰

Baird was also aware that even in waters that seem to be clean and sparkling blue, dolphins and whales face another deadly form of pollution: man-made underwater noise. Incredibly loud sounds clang and roar and hum through the ocean at all times, coming from ships, military training, oil drilling, dredging, and undersea construction, among other sources. Scientists refer to this as acoustic smog, and they estimate that its levels have risen tenfold over the past twenty-five years. In other words, the oceans are becoming *much* noisier. This din makes things extremely difficult for dolphins and whales, who rely on their hearing for hunting, mating, avoiding predators, navigating, migrating, communicating—really, for everything in their lives. As they try to escape the constant noise, or struggle to cope with it, they become chronically stressed and sick.

If our environment were flooded with these levels of noise, we wouldn't survive for long. We would desperately try to flee from it—but dolphins and whales have nowhere to go. The noise is everywhere. For a sense of how insanely loud the ocean has become, consider these numbers: Ships rumble by at about 180 decibels (units that indicate the intensity of sound) below the surface. At 185 decibels, human eardrums will burst; 200-decibel shock waves will blow a cow off its feet and cause death on land. The most deafening underwater noise comes from the air guns used by oil companies to prospect the seafloor. These guns—which are towed behind boats and blasted every ten seconds for months at a time—register at 250 decibels, louder than an atomic bomb exploding. (Noise this earsplitting harms all creatures exposed to it, across vast areas of ocean.) The most relentless source of underwater noise is military training. Sonar is the US Navy's main tool, used to detect the presence of enemy submarines or other underwater threats, but it is also one of the loudest noises in the sea: 236 decibels, about the intensity of a rocket launch. In areas where underwater war games have occurred, with navy sonar being deployed, dolphins and whales have stranded in groups with blood streaming out of their ears and eyes.

Though military sonar is proven to hurt cetaceans, the navy has battled all the way to the Supreme Court to avoid even the slightest restrictions on where and when it unleashes its sonic weaponry. In fact, the military has submitted new proposals to greatly increase its sonar use. Its plans called for 500,000 hours of sonar operations and the detonation of 260,000 explosives in Hawaiian and Southern Californian waters alone. By the navy's own estimates, this bombardment would result in 155 dolphin and whale deaths, along with 2,000 serious permanent injuries, and almost ten million instances of hearing loss and disruptions of vital behaviors.

These days, a major part of Baird's work involves placing satellite tags on the dolphins and whales who frequent the depths, where they are more at risk from sonar exposure. The tags track the dolphins' movements with precision. Baird can log on to his computer to see how the tagged animals react to military activities, which are widespread in Hawaii. He had already established the existence of resident melon-head whale, false killer whale, pygmy killer whale, and pilot whale populations around the islands—all deep dwellers who are highly sensitive to noise—and recommended that their turf be spared from aggressive sonar use and live missile tests. He had tagged 218 dolphins and whales, and watched them adapt (or not) to the underwater noise around them.

That might sound simple, but the deepwater dolphins don't give up their secrets easily. Baird's work takes a lot of patience. "One of my long-term interests is, how do you study animals that spend most of their time underwater?" he said. On an average day, Baird leaves the marina at sunrise, returns in the late afternoon, and covers a hundred miles in a small boat. The best way for me to understand his research, he told me, would be to accompany his team on a field project.

〜〜〜〜

"If I didn't warn you, we spend a lot of time just cruising around."

Baird sat on the bridge of his twenty-seven-foot Boston Whaler, piloting us toward the southern tip of the Big Island. We were a few miles offshore; the calm conditions were ideal for sighting the little disturbances that might be a dolphin's dorsal fin—even the blip of a fish breaking the surface was visible from afar. From the start, the day had been hot, the sky layered with wispy clouds that only seemed to intensify the sun's glare.

Daniel Webster, Baird's right hand colleague, stood at the bow. Webster was athletic and nimble, his brown hair tucked under a baseball cap. He was quiet but quick to smile, and I could tell instantly that he was a pro. There is a high degree of difficulty to performing intricate tasks on a tiny, rocking boat, but Webster managed it with humor and ease. One of his most challenging jobs was tagging the dolphins when they poked their heads above water—often for only a second or two—while Baird positioned the boat. This was about as easy as hitting an archery bull's-eye while balancing on one foot, on a conveyor belt.

Facing Webster, scouting the expanse of ocean behind him, was biologist Brenda Rone. Rone specialized in difficult whale assignments. She worked often in the cold, stormy waters off Alaska and the Arctic, searching for blue whales, right whales, bowheads, and humpbacks, maneuvering to tag their massive, rolling bodies. Today, she leaned against the whaler's windshield, eyes hidden behind polarized sunglasses, blond hair pulled back in a ponytail. Rounding out the crew was Kelly Beach, an intern from Baird's group, the Cascadia Research Collective, in Olympia, Washington.

Photography was a key part of the work. Stacked behind Rone were hard-sided cases containing Canon cameras with zoom lenses. Encounters with rare dolphins were fast and furious, and the most important thing, aside from tagging, was to document the animals when they showed themselves. Later, back on land, the scientists would pore over the pictures and extract information from them: who was still around, who was missing, who had a new calf or a fresh dorsal fin injury, who was looking skinny. With so few sightings of these rare species, every detail mattered.

Because it was my first day I was seated next to Baird on the bridge, shaded from the merciless sun. My job, not very demanding, was to hit a clicker whenever anyone spotted a wedge-tailed shearwater or a Bulwer's petrel, two seabird species. When any other bird whizzed overhead, Baird yelled out, "Photo!" calling the species on the fly: "Black-winged petrel!" Webster hung his body over the rail, his camera whirring on motor drive. While cruising, Baird noted everything, even the tiniest movements on the water. The team also stopped to pick up bobbing trash— and there was a lot of it. The most common floating objects were balloons, which are deadly. Turtles, dolphins, and other marine animals eat them, mistaking them for fish or squid, with fatal results.

We motored slowly south, to avoid the trade winds. The light turned a silvery yellow, with clouds massing above the volcano peaks. Webster came and sat with Baird and me on the bridge, because there wasn't much happening on the water. We stopped to net a dead squid, its body bitten in half, and we saw frigate birds gliding overhead, and some fish hopping around, but no dolphins. "We see false killer whales about once every three weeks," Webster said. Baird nodded: "That's why, historically, there hasn't been a lot of research on the species. But we try to be productive the rest of the time. We'll work with whatever we find out here."

To increase his odds of finding these elusive dolphins, Baird had created field guides he left with boat captains, tour operators, scuba clubs—anyone who might stumble across a pod of false killer whales. The guides were beautifully designed and crammed with information, with Baird's cell phone number placed prominently on each page. Outreach is key, Baird noted, when you hope to raise concern for a creature that most people have never heard of, and will probably never see. He had even created false killer whale press-on tattoos, which he passed out to kids to get them more interested in the species.

I had wondered what it was about false killer whales that Baird loved so much, and as we were driving, I asked him. He brightened; there were few things he liked to talk about more. The thing about these animals that surprises people, he told me, is that they are as fascinated by us as we are by them: "They recognize humans as being something similar to them."

Two colleagues of Baird's, Dan McSweeney and Deron Verbeck, had spent time in the water with false killer whales, both men returning with awesome stories of the encounters. One time, McSweeney was diving near a pod when one of the whales swam up to him with a tuna in its mouth and passed it to him, as though delivering a gift. He took it; the whale swam away and then boomeranged back. McSweeney handed the fish to the whale, who once again took it gently in his mouth. "It's not the first time this kind of thing has been documented," Baird said. "It's basically ritualistic prey sharing. I say ritualistic because I think it has a symbolic component to it."

While other top predators like sharks and lions often share their prey, jointly ripping into whatever they'd caught, Baird had observed false killer whales passing a fish among themselves, without anyone taking the slightest nibble. "I don't know of any other species that does this," he said. "So why would they? Well, they're hunting buddies. They've probably been hunting together for years. It's a way of demonstrating trust. And the fact that they give it back . . . it's not like they're trying to get more of the fish themselves. The purpose of this isn't just to eat the prey. There's something more: it's part of their culture. And you know, what's going on in the head of an animal that actually brings food to another species?" He laughed. "I have a dog. He's really cute. But when I give him a bone, he's certainly not going to offer it to me."

〰〰〰

The sky the next morning was pink and windless, and we chugged out of the marina promptly at dawn. Before long we ran into a pod of bottlenose dolphins. Baird idled the engine so we could take photos.

The bottlenoses swam up to the boat, game for a little wake riding. Their bodies looked emerald green below the water. Standing on the bow, I could see them closely. Many of the dolphins were marked with scrapes and cookiecutter shark bites, round wounds and scars on their bodies. One dolphin's dorsal fin had been lopped in half.

I was struck by how powerful the bottlenoses looked, and how curious they were about everything around them. I would have happily watched them for hours, but Webster suddenly pointed in front of us. *Kogia!* he shouted. This meant nothing to me, but everyone else snapped to attention. A black back broke the surface, followed by a blunt head. Whatever it was, there were three of them. The animals disappeared quickly, but Baird had seen enough

157

to confirm the sighting: dwarf sperm whales (*kogia* is their Latin name). "This is one of the species that's sensitive to navy sonar," he said, with a frown. "It's an extremely poorly known species. We've got a hundred and fifteen individuals in our catalog, and it's the only long-term study in existence."

We waited for almost an hour, but the whales didn't show themselves again. These particular creatures, Baird noted, are tough to track. They stay down a long time between breaths and are skilled at shaking observers off their tails: "There's no relationship between the way they're traveling when they dive and where they come up. Often they'll go in a completely different direction."

Webster dropped the hydrophone, an underwater listening device that enabled us to hear the dolphin and whale chatter below. It bobbed in the water, an orange flag signaling its location. If any cetaceans were around, this would pick up their clicks and whistles and buzzes. In the realms below forty or fifty feet, light ebbs quickly, so sound is far more important than vision. And the ocean is a great conductor: sound travels 4.3 times faster in water than it does in air. Zipping around in the darkness down there, dolphins and whales would be lost without their echolocation. Sound is their compass.

The discovery that certain animals navigate their worlds by relying on sound rather than vision dates back to 1773, when an Italian scientist named Lazzaro Spallanzani noticed that bats could fly expertly in total darkness, swerving around obstacles they couldn't possibly see. Puzzled by this, Spallanzani caught some bats and began to experiment with them.

You would not have wanted to be one of Spallanzani's bats. Though his first experiment was sort of cute—he outfitted the creatures in tiny hoods—Spallanzani quickly moved on to heavier-handed efforts, blinding them and even removing their eyes, coating their bodies in varnish and flour paste. But once the bats recovered from their injuries, they could still hunt with ease, even eyeless. Spallanzani was stumped. He moved on to their ears, plugging them with hot wax. This time, success: the bats bumped into things. Without their hearing, it seemed, they were lost. When Spallanzani presented his findings, suggesting that bats were sonic geniuses without much use for their other senses, he was laughed at by some of the most renowned scientists of his day. His theory was ignored for a century, referred to dismissively as "Spallanzani's Bat Problem."

But Spallanzani was right. He had discovered the phenomenon of animals that could echolocate, or produce their own biological sonar. He had proven this with his bats. It wasn't until 1947 that another scientist figured out that dolphins could echolocate, too. (By this point, of course, dolphins had been echolocating for about thirty-five million years.)

Basically, echolocation—or sonar—involves sending out a beam of sound and then analyzing the returning echoes to determine the physical properties of an object in space, or underwater. Different materials reflect sound at different wavelengths. Some items are bouncy and send back a strong signal. Others absorb sound, and the echoes are weaker. All sonar systems consist of three parts: a transmitter, a receiver, and a way to process the signals.

Scientists soon learned that dolphin sonar is fine-tuned beyond belief. The animals beam ultrasonic clicks out of their foreheads, using a fat-filled sac called a melon to focus the sound. They receive the echoes through their lower jaws, which are also lined with fatty liquids. From the jaws, the acoustic feedback is transmitted up to their ears and into their brain, where it's interpreted and relayed to other senses, such as vision.

When the dolphins make their clicks, they come out in a stream of sound, up to two thousand clicks per second. Here is the most astonishing part: dolphins can aim and adjust each click *individually,* changing direction, volume, and frequency—a feat of unimaginable precision. They can even send out two click streams at once, in different directions, at varying frequencies. Using this sense, dolphins can detect microscopic differences in the size or composition of identical-looking objects, even at a distance. It's a spectacular system, exquisitely adapted to life underwater. When man-made noises flood the dolphins' environment, it's like us being blinded by light so bright that we can't see anything. But sound creates pressure waves—battering walls of energy—so for a more accurate comparison, add to that our heads painfully exploding in the glare.

~~~~~

The next day, we hit the deepwater dolphin jackpot: Baird got a tip from a sportfishing captain who had seen a pod of three hundred melon-headed whales. We found the whales about twelve miles offshore, and they approached the boat, eager to play, spyhopping, buzzing us, and hanging out at the surface in bunches. The melon-heads were smallish, with round heads and cute little beaks. They had an endearing presence. "They love to surf," Baird said. "When you accelerate even a little bit, you'll get twenty of them riding the bow."

Melon-heads often travel in large groups, and they appeared delighted with one another's company. A pod of rough-toothed dolphins had joined them, and weaving among all the dorsal fins were two sharks, an oceanic whitetip and a silky shark, their slinky bodies visible at the surface. The rough-toothed dolphins liked to jump, pogoing high in the air, and they had patches of pink on their skin, and long, narrow beaks. They looked almost prehistoric, but with some serious athletic skills.

The pods stayed with the boat for hours, everyone gunning their cameras. Baird called out directions to help Webster aim his tagging gun, which resembled a miniature crossbow, as hundreds of dolphins darted around us and under us. (The last thing anyone wanted to see was a $5,000 satellite tag missing its mark and sinking into the deep.)

"They're flippy little dudes," Rone said, with a smile. Webster nodded, wiping sweat from his forehead. "There'll be nothing, nothing, nothing," he said, "and then—mass chaos!" One melon-head swam alongside the boat, right where I was standing, and opened his mouth, as though he were laughing. Watching him, I imagined that he was talking and joking as merrily as someone at an excellent party.

The wind had kicked up some waves, and the boat rocked from side to side. We were far enough offshore, I realized, that we might see anything, even sperm whales, the largest toothed whales of all. (After being hunted for centuries this species is now endangered, but Hawaii is home to a small population.) Or beaked whales, odd-looking creatures who spend most of their time in the depths. If we were terrifically lucky, we might even see orcas. Killer whale sightings are rare in Hawaii—Baird had encountered them here only a few times. In 2013, he managed to tag three orcas from a pod of seven, and another researcher had photographed one of the orcas swimming along with a shark sticking out of her mouth like a toothpick.

≈≈≈≈

Orcas are unusual animals. At a glance they all look alike, but that is misleading. In many cases, orca clans are so distinct from one another that scientists suspect they are actually separate species. In the Pacific Northwest alone, there are three types of orcas, commonly referred to as residents, transients, and offshores. Killer whales from each of these groups have about as much in common as investment bankers, rock stars, and farmers. The residents prefer to eat Chinook salmon, choosing to go hungry rather than settle for other fish. The transients hunt seals and sea lions and won't touch salmon of any kind. Offshore orcas like to dine on sharks, expertly fileting the liver. There is no overlap between these tribes, and they actively avoid one another. If they do make contact, there can be scuffles. When two pods from the same clan meet up, however, they may greet each other in an elaborate ceremony.

To our ears, orca vocalizations sound like a spooky ghost choir, unearthly cries that all blend together, but scientists analyzing these calls have discovered that each pod has its own dialect. Different types of orcas also have different styles of communication. Residents make a lot of noise while they hunt. Transients are stealthily silent, celebrating loudly only after they've fed. Offshore orcas slap their tails while they are swimming, for reasons nobody knows. All three groups use their echolocation with individual flair. Even their striking markings are not a one-size-fits-all orca uniform: across the oceans, the details of killer whales' body sizes, fin shapes, and white patches vary widely.

As recently as the sixties, orcas were viewed as extremely dangerous animals—which is how they got their intimidating name: killer whales. The larger males were dominant, people believed, and would attack us if given the chance. They were called "the biggest confirmed man-eaters in the ocean," and the "tigers of the sea." But soon, as scientists began to study the orcas, they realized how wrong this menacing image was.

Despite plenty of opportunity and provocation, orcas have never killed a single person anywhere in the world's seas. (By comparison, in 2014 dogs killed forty-two people in America alone.) Orcas are top predators who show gentle curiosity toward us, expert communicators who demonstrate complex wisdom. In their society, it's not the males who are dominant. It's the female orcas, or matriarchs, who control their pods—especially the oldest grannies. Throughout their entire lives, orcas stick close to their mommas. An orca's pod is his immediate family, a group that might contain four generations. Each pod is part of a bigger clan, also made up of close relations, and at the top of the orca organizational chart are the larger communities, made up of clans—what we would call nations.

A killer whale's life education unfolds at a pace that is similar to ours. They learn socially, like we do, and nothing happens instantly. Maturity comes over time. At twenty years old, orcas are still learning and growing. Matriarchs have been known to live past one hundred, often outlasting their offspring.

This blue planet we live on? It's had oceans for 3.8 billion years. In an aquatic realm where history isn't written down in books, it is the matriarch who carries the information, everything her pod needs to survive into the future. She is the keeper of the dialect. She teaches her descendants their very identity. She shows everyone how to hunt, which is no small task when you consider the tricky and specialized techniques that orcas use. In Argentina, one group makes the high stakes move of purposely stranding themselves—rocketing onto the beach, grabbing a seal, and then hopefully propelling themselves back into the water. Scientists have watched young orcas being coached for six years before they even attempt this.

Depending on where he lives, an orca might learn to blow bubble curtains to herd fish, or pop his head above water to identify a delicious species of seal. He may need to learn fast-moving formations that would challenge the Hogwarts Quidditch team, working with his pod in a three-dimensional, life-or-death match against sperm whales. He might practice pulling up stingrays from a muddy seafloor (without getting stung), or be shown how to immobilize a great white shark, flipping it upside down and then holding it there until it drowns. None of these are simple or easy moves.

The matriarch also knows *where* to hunt, and when. As the climate changes, the ocean changes in radical ways, too. This year's excellent hunting grounds might be empty the next year. When circumstances change for the orcas, the matriarch is the key to the pod's survival. Using everything she knows, she'll figure out plan B.

Sometimes when they're describing what's so special about orcas, scientists become emotional. One marine biologist called them "the most amazing animals that currently live on our planet." Another scientist named them the unchallenged rulers of the world's oceans. Among people who have encountered orcas, this level of enthusiasm is expressed often, in language usually reserved for five-star movie reviews.

At the end of the day, we came across two more dolphin species: spotted dolphins and pilot whales. One of the spotted dolphins veered off from his pod and headed toward us to check out the boat. I could see that the tip of his beak was white, its silvery color scuffed like he'd been in a fight. Another dolphin followed him; this one had a remora stuck on his head, right below his eye. Remoras, the suckerfish that hitchhike along on dolphins' bodies, look innocent enough, but it's clear they cause some pain. Looking closer, I could see blood seeping out of the dolphin's skin.

These sightings brought our total to six dolphin species in two days: pretty great. But of course, we hadn't found the false killer whales. But maybe someone else had. For Baird, the definition of a good day is one on which *somebody* crosses paths with these mysterious dolphins, and manages to take half-decent pictures of them. It doesn't have to be him—it's the sighting itself that is precious. When people send him their photos, Baird can extract all kinds of information from them.

A few weeks after I got home, Baird emailed to tell me there had been a major false killer whale sighting near the Big Island—a pod of thirty animals, including some calves. And even better, the people who encountered them happened to be a group of professional underwater photographers. The resulting videos and pictures were so fantastic that they ended up on the Hawaiian evening news.

Watching the footage, I could see why this was Baird's favorite species. The false killer whales whizzed around the divers, buzzing them joyfully. It was quite a scene: the world's rarest dolphins swooping in for their close-ups, their clicks and whistles echoing through a blue cathedral of sea. One of the whales swam up to the camera, stopped, stared into the lens, and then made some loud creaking sounds that made him seem like he was asking a question.

Will we ever be able to understand what the dolphins are saying? It's a tantalizing thought. After all, they are individuals, speaking to us in distinct voices. We know they have names, so it seems likely they have ways to describe other things, too. Are they talking about their feelings? Their plans? Their dreams? Are they telling silly jokes? Revealing secrets from the deep? Who knows? But in a perfect world, their voices would be the only sounds we would hear echoing through the ocean.

Chapter 9

Thera

≈≈≈

The oldest dolphins in the world were born 3,800 years ago, when a prehistoric artist in Greece sat down, picked up his brush, and painted them leaping across the side of a rough clay bowl. Almost four millennia later, those dolphins still look lively. They are the earliest images of the animals known to us, ancient evidence of the bond between humans and dolphins. The artist did not sign his name and he came from a long-lost civilization, so we don't know much about him. But one thing is obvious: whoever painted these dolphins did so with affection.

I stepped back so I could see the dolphins in their museum display case. They were painted in black and white, on a red clay bowl about the size and shape of a breadbasket.

If you didn't know the origin of this bowl, you might find it kind of boring. After all, it's only a humble kitchen utensil. The Athens National Archaeological Museum is where people go to look at grand marble statues of thunderbolt-hurling, superhero Greek gods—not pottery covered in whimsical little dolphins. Learning the story of these dolphins, however, would change your mind. This pod's place in history is important, and the tale that accompanies them is one of humanity's greatest riddles.

I'd arrived in Athens the previous day, landing in a depressed country. Greece was stuck in an economic crisis. The streets were dirty, covered in graffiti. Every other storefront was boarded up and out of business; stray dogs prowled the streets. Even in the museum, one of the world's finest collections, here and there the lights were burnt out, giving the building an air of neglect. I walked through galleries filled with magnificent statues, memorials to classical Greek history—but I had come to see the dolphins. They were tucked into a small room on the second floor, the Thera Gallery. You could easily miss it, which was somehow fitting: the Minoans, the people whose artworks filled this gallery, eluded us for more than three thousand years.

At the height of their civilization, around 1700 BC, the Minoans had lived around the Cyclades, a group of islands in the Aegean Sea. Their main strongholds were Crete and

Thera (now known as Santorini), but their influence was felt all the way to Asia, Africa, and possibly beyond. They were master seafarers, ocean people, celestial navigators who sailed over the horizon at a time long before maps. The purpose of their voyages was trade. Luxurious Minoan goods—fine pottery, gold jewelry, bronze tools, olive oil, an intoxicating drink they'd invented called wine—were coveted by even the Egyptian pharaohs. As a result, the Minoans were wealthy, and they built palaces that were dripping in beauty. They were confident, too: unusually, none of their settlements were fortified against invaders. As a sophisticated people with roots reaching back to the Stone Age, you'd think the Minoans would be as familiar to us as the Egyptians, the Romans, the Persians, or the ancient Greeks. But they aren't. Instead, they are shadowy figures in history, and their existence is one long string of question marks.

Maybe it's easy to disappear when you're buried under a hundred feet of ash, which is how their culture met its end. Sometime around 1500 BC, an epic volcanic explosion on Thera snuffed out the bright spark of Minoan life. This eruption was unlike anything in history. It was four times more violent than Krakatoa, the Indonesian volcano that exploded in 1883, partially collapsed, and killed thirty-six thousand people. When Thera's volcano blew its top, it belched clouds of smoke, gas, and rock miles into the air. It blotted out the sun, darkening the sky for months. Its roar was heard in Africa; its ashes fell in Asia. The island's peaks heaved and shuddered, crashing into the sea, kicking up a towering tsunami. Palaces and cities were destroyed—many people believe that Thera inspired the mythical story of Atlantis. No one knows exactly what happened to the Minoans after that, but by 1400 BC they were gone, replaced by the warlike Mycenaeans.

The Minoans had vanished so completely that it was only by chance that archeologists found them. To date, researchers have dug up thousands of artworks and several major settlements—but it is still only a fraction of the Minoans' heritage. What we have discovered so far is incredible: brightly colored, highly detailed paintings and frescoes (paintings made on wet plaster walls), along with ceramics, sculptures, jewelry, and architecture. Many of the paintings depict joyful-looking, athletic people playing and celebrating. One figure who shows up often, painted with great care, is the goddess Potnia, the mistress of the animals. In exquisite frescoes and gold seals, she is shown dancing in olive groves with her priestesses, with lions at her heel and dolphins cradled in her arms. What's missing in Minoan art is also important: there are absolutely no images of war, or fighting, or any kind of violence. And though the Minoans were prosperous and lacked nothing, there are also no images or suggestions of money.

Among the most famous Minoan artifacts are a series of frescoes found on Thera, in a seaside city known as Akrotiri. When the volcano erupted, Akrotiri was buried deep in ash and pumice, and it stayed that way until 1967, when a Greek archaeologist named Spyridon Marinatos began to peel away the layers of earth. He uncovered two- and three-story houses with comforts nobody expected to find in a prehistoric settlement: the Minoans even had running hot water. During the volcanic explosion, the people had fled—no human remains have turned up—but they left behind hundreds of artworks. In many buildings the walls were covered with murals, done in the Minoans' distinctive, graceful style. They featured beautifully dressed women bending to touch flowers, birds kissing in the air, dolphins and monkeys playing, spirals painted in vibrant colors. Marinatos also found many household possessions, including the dolphin pottery I'd seen in Athens.

Taken as a snapshot of the Minoans—what they cared about, how they lived—the artworks tell a riveting story, with dolphins among the key players. Other ancient cultures had close relationships with dolphins, too, but their tales have been passed down in songs and chants, so they seem more like myths than true accounts. The West African Dogon people, for instance, claim their ancestors were dolphinlike beings called Nommos, who descended to earth from Sirius, a star system in the constellation Canis Major. In the Amazon, many people believe that the river's pink dolphins, or botos, are clever sorcerers who often appear on land disguised as handsome men, looking to date women. The botos are messengers from another realm, the Amazon shamans say, guides between this world and an underwater world called the Encante, where everything shines like diamonds. The idea that dolphins can morph into humans whenever they want is also found in Aboriginal Australian legends, Pacific Island chants, Native American folklore, and Greek epic poems. These tales, whether they're true or not, reflect a deep connection between our two species. But while other cultures talked about their bond with dolphins, only the Minoans provided actual proof. Dolphins show up all over their world. If there were any people who painted dolphins earlier, or more often, or more brilliantly than the Minoans, we haven't found them. So who were these playful, peaceful dolphin lovers—and what are they whispering to us from so long ago?

≈≈≈≈

Thera was the most dramatic place I'd ever seen, and it stirred my imagination. Coming in on the ferry, I gasped when the island came into view. Where there had once been an almost perfectly round landmass, now there was a ragged crescent of volcanic rock banded in layers of rust, brown, and gray. It was as though a chunk of the place had been clawed away by a giant paw and flung into the sea. Inside the caldera, the 1,200-foot-deep pit left by the eruption, the water lay as still as black marble.

I had immediately set out to explore, walking narrow paths shared by surefooted donkeys. All of Thera faced the sea, its buildings clinging to sheer cliffs that plunged to the water. If you slipped here, you would fall for a mile. In the pretty town of Oia, I found dolphins everywhere: stenciled on walls, stamped onto hotel signs, etched into jewelry, painted on pots that were replicas of Minoan designs.

The sun was setting, and people had gathered along pathways to watch its descent. I walked past an old man sitting at a rickety table, leaning against the wall of his whitewashed house. *"Kalimera,"* I said, using the only Greek word I knew. "Hello." He smiled and motioned for me to join him. My feet were sore and he looked like he might have been here long enough to have personally known some Minoans, so I sat down. Though he didn't speak a word of English, that didn't stop us from having a conversation. He pointed to the glowing sunset and touched his heart. I nodded and did the same. Then I drew a dolphin on a scrap of paper and handed it to him. "Ah," he said, "Akrotiri!" I nodded. Using sign language, I told him that I was planning to visit Akrotiri the next day.

My timing was lucky. Until recently Akrotiri had been off-limits, closed for eight years after a tourist died when part of the excavation's roof caved in. The site had just reopened, and now the town that had produced so many brilliant Minoan artworks was once again accessible to see. I had read everything I could find about Akrotiri, and I knew that my dolphin investigations needed to start in its abandoned streets.

What did I hope to find there? As the night rose up from the caldera, I thought about this. I suppose I wanted to know how the Minoans, a powerful, wealthy people, had managed to live in harmony with nature—for thousands of years. In the modern world, armed with mighty technologies, we have chosen another route. We believe that we're in charge of everything on this earth, and nature is ours to do with as we please. We use plants and animals and ecosystems in any way that suits us, however destructive or cruel or shortsighted our actions may be. There is nothing we won't mess with, even our own genetic code.

Not long before I'd come to Greece, scientists released a paper estimating that half the world's animals have been exterminated in only two generations—and that's before you consider what has happened to plants and insects, coral reefs and rain forests and other ecosystems. Right now, humanity is causing extinctions at a terrifying rate. We *know* we are mowing down life—we've made charts and graphs and we count everything on spreadsheets—but that understanding hasn't stopped us from doing it. The oceans and deserts, forests and mountains, lakes and rivers, tundras and glaciers, plants and animals, they are all dying on our watch.

What was it about the Minoans that made them embrace nature—especially the ocean—rather than fearing it, exploiting it, or trying to conquer it, like every other civilization that followed them? And whatever it was, could we learn to do it, too? Why were dolphins given such a prominent place in their world, along with other creatures: birds, bees, bulls, snakes, lions, and octopi appear often in their art. Trees were another favorite subject, and so were flowers. And what about the Minoan fascination with spirals? They drew that symbol everywhere. What did these things mean to them—and what, after all these years, should they mean to us?

≈≈≈≈

Akrotiri was a city of ash, layers and layers of pale gray ash. The buildings were still partially buried, braced with scaffolding so you could walk around them and peer into their rooms. Large ceramic urns were strewn on the ground, some of them tipped on their sides. I was awed by Akrotiri, and judging from the expressions on other people's faces, this was a typical response. The sight of a buried city is one you can never really prepare for, or easily make sense of. Which is where my guide, Lefteris Zorzos, came in.

Zorzos was the youngest archaeologist ever to work at Akrotiri, beginning his lifelong devotion to the site in 1999, at age sixteen. In his research, Zorzos had identified thirty Minoan archaeological sites around Thera, and that was just for starters. "There's quite a bit underneath everything we're standing on," he told me. "When the eruption happened, it wasn't just Akrotiri that was preserved—the entire island was preserved."

The day was as hot as lava, but under the climate-controlled roof the air was cool and dry. When he began to dig, Spyridon Marinatos had realized that Akrotiri was such a significant place that the entire archaeological site should be turned into a museum. The Greek government had enclosed the ruins in a building and done what it could to protect the Minoan treasures, but the country's economic crisis had put a stop to the work. "There hasn't been an excavation in several years," Zorzos said, with regret in his voice. "Very little research, very little conservation. So we are fighting on a local level to get things going." Often, he told me, he paid for Akrotiri's expenses out of his own pocket: "In 2000, we had a hundred archaeologists working here. Now we have just four or five guards. You can imagine the difference."

We stood near the entrance on an elevated floor that was level with the top stories of the buildings. The site was large, but Zorzos estimated it was only about 3 percent of Akrotiri's full footprint. This had been a busy place, home to thousands of people, perched by the sea like a Minoan San Francisco or Sydney. No one knows where the city's boundaries lie. Part of the settlement might be underwater now, or it might rest farther inland, still hidden under the ground.

Most of Akrotiri's buildings were private houses, Zorzos said, but a few had the grand appearance of public gathering spaces. "What we're seeing is the urban center," he pointed out. "And if you look below, you can see the sewer system running underneath the street level. It was a very, very advanced—*very advanced*—society."

The archaeologists were stunned to find that the walls of almost every structure were covered with vibrant Minoan frescoes, and these paintings had survived under the ash. Pottery of all shapes and sizes filled the houses, decorated with spirals and flowers and birds and dolphins;

some buildings had floors that shimmered with crushed seashells. Akrotiri's aquatic spirit and its location at the water's edge made it a perfect place for Minoans and dolphins to have met.

As we walked around, Zorzos pointed out how the layers of ash and rock corresponded to the phases of the eruption. When Thera's volcano first exploded, it spewed out a coarse pumice, followed by a torrential silvery hail. At some point, boulders had been ejected like cannonballs, crashing through walls, and they could still be seen, lying where they'd landed. Early in the destruction, the temperature inside Akrotiri hit three hundred degrees Celsius. Then things got even hotter: "The second phase was four hundred degrees," Zorzos said. "So you're talking about complete annihilation."

He showed me a building called the West House next. It contained so many ocean-themed artworks that researchers believed it had been the home of an admiral or a ship captain. "This is probably one of the most important buildings in the Mediterranean," Zorzos said. In his first assignment at Akrotiri he had excavated a clay pipe on its ground floor, part of an efficient, anti-erosion drainage system. There was also a stone toilet that flushed, the earliest ever found.

The West House rose three stories high, with a wide

stone staircase connecting the floors. Each floor had large windows that looked out on a triangular town square. The top floor had been wrapped in a thirty-nine-foot-long fresco of Thera's sailing fleet. Its panels show a red sand beach that still exists next to Akrotiri, with seven ships and many smaller boats circling the harbor. The city is drawn in great detail, filled with people dressed for a party. Personally, what I noticed first were the festive pods of dolphins. They were everywhere, painted in blue, scarlet, rust, and gold, leaping over the ships, escorting the fleet, and in some cases, even mingling with the crowds on shore.

Zorzos had saved one corner for last, a huge three-story building known as Xeste 3. It had been constructed with blocks of volcanic stone, fitted together as tightly as puzzle pieces. "They had ingenious ways of keeping these tall buildings upright," he explained. "Every floor is built slightly farther inward to make it stable. I've discussed it with architects—what you're seeing is very difficult to do even with cement today." Archaeologists believed that Xeste 3 had been used for a sacred purpose—that it was a place with special intrigue. Considering what they found inside it, this was an excellent guess.

The lower two floors are a maze of rooms, at least one of which was sunken, and probably used for cleansing or bathing. But the building's most striking feature was its artwork: in Xeste 3, *every* vertical surface had been painted with frescoes. These astonishing pieces had been carefully removed and transferred to a workshop on site, where they are restored over years before being loaned to museums. This process is closed to the public, but Zorzos had arranged for me to see it. In particular, he wanted to show me the frescoes from Xeste 3's top floor. "I will not say any more," he said, with a grin. "Seeing them ... well, I don't think you will believe what you see." He checked his watch and nodded. "So let's go. I think we are ready."

~~~~~~

We walked over to a workshop behind the archeological site, where the frescoes are kept. One of the restorers, a woman named Litsa, greeted us at the door and showed us into the building. Litsa was petite, maybe five feet tall and a hundred pounds, and most of it was her smile. She leaned her whole body into the task of pulling the first twelve-foot-square fresco out on its rollers, digging in with her silver sneakers. I gasped when I saw the painting, and Zorzos smiled because he was expecting my reaction. It was an enormous portrait of Potnia.

The goddess was breathtakingly lovely. She was seated in profile, leaning forward so you could see her long black ponytail dotted with rubies cascading down her back. She wore a necklace of dragonflies, and earrings like gold moons. Crocuses, the symbol of spring, were embroidered on her flowing dress. Below her, appearing as smaller figures, were a girl and a blue monkey. The fresco's colors—crimson, navy, gold, ivory, white, black—were as vivid as if they had been painted yesterday. When the Minoans came to worship, they had climbed to the top floor of Xeste 3, and this is whom they expected to find. This lady represented everything to them. She was Mother Nature, in human form.

"The level of detail is incredible," Zorzos said in a whisper. "You can see it in her hands. Her fingernails are painted; her hair is very elaborate. Her dress itself is absolutely spectacular—there is an actual landscape on it: swallows, lilies, everything together. It has a lot of energy and power."

The next panels Litsa pulled out were enormous blue spirals that had also come from Xeste 3's top floor, sitting above the goddess. Looking at them, I was speechless. The Minoans, it seemed, were determined to immerse themselves in beauty and wonder. Everything about them was exotic and mysterious.

Researchers believe the Minoans' spirals represent a circular view of time, as opposed to the linear one we've adopted. In their outlook, birth, life, death, and rebirth exist in a continuous cycle—like the phases of the moon, and the changing of seasons. To the Minoans, life was not a one-way street that just ended one day: it wound on forever, and throughout all of it nature supported them. And the dolphins who popped up so often were the guides from this world to the underworld, and then back again.

This may seem like a lot of guesswork, but to me it all rang true. Anyone could see that even the simplest Minoan objects reflected a deep love of nature. In the modern world, we've chosen money and technology over flowers or butterflies or dolphins. Our relationship with nature is way out of balance—but perhaps we can fix it. Maybe it's not too late for us to summon some of the Minoan joy and love. I wondered if Zorzos, who had spent so much time among their ghosts, had picked up on their vibe. Walking around Akrotiri late at night, for instance, had he ever sensed the Minoans' presence?

"Yes," he said, "but it's hard to describe."

"Is it a good feeling?" I asked, probing.

Zorzos smiled slowly. "Yes," he said. "Definitely, yes."

The road was ordinary, running slightly uphill from Crete's dreary capital city, Heraklion. Along its route there were markets and T-shirt shops and car-repair joints, the usual

185

stuff, nothing to indicate that if you followed this road it would lead you directly to a dazzling Minoan palace called Knossos.

In the late nineteenth century, archaeologists had become interested in some fields set among Crete's low-lying hills: farmers and shepherds had been tripping over scraps of pottery and the tops of buried walls in this area for years. There was something down there, the archaeologists realized, something *big*. A wealthy British man named Sir Arthur Evans stepped in and bought the land. He started to dig in 1900.

It was an exciting time to hunt for lost civilizations. A German archaeologist named Heinrich Schliemann had just found the ancient Greek cities of Troy and Mycenae, rewriting history and hauling up tons of gold. Just about anybody willing to pick up a shovel could find something old and incredible in the ground. When Evans first visited Crete, he was shocked to find the local women wearing necklaces of gemstones they'd collected in the fields. Walking around the area, Evans himself had stubbed his toe on a clay tablet covered with inscriptions, carved in a language that no one had ever seen before.

(This Minoan language is now known as Linear A, and to this day it remains a mystery. Many scholars have tried to translate it; none have succeeded. More examples of this writing would be found on Crete and Thera, including the Phaistos Disc, a circle of fired clay about the size and shape of a mini pizza. The disc is stamped 241 times with symbols arranged in a spiral on both sides. Some of the symbols are familiar: a bird in flight, a woman in a long skirt, a man's head, an oar, a beehive, a leafy branch, a snake. Others are unknown. But there is one thing I can tell you for sure about the Phaistos Disc: the symbol of a dolphin appears on it five times.)

Having secured his site, Evans began to dig—and what lay beneath the fields proved to be even more amazing than anyone had suspected: a vast complex of buildings, filled with the Minoans' signature artworks. One of his most celebrated finds was a long fresco of dolphins, painted underwater as though the artist had been down there with them. I wondered how the Minoans would have known what the dolphins were doing below the surface. But then I read that Evans had turned up Minoan magnifying lenses and mirrors made of crystal—maybe they had underwater masks, too. It was clear these artists had observed the dolphins in action.

I'd been warned that Knossos would be jammed with sightseers, so I arrived early in the morning, but I still found myself lining up for a ticket behind busloads of people. It was a sweltering day and tourists milled at the entrance, fanning themselves. Guides wearing earpieces held signs aloft and attempted to herd their groups; vendors hawking Knossos posters, tote bags, and fridge magnets swarmed outside the gates.

I decided to do the tour backward, so I would be free of the crowds until at least the halfway point. Knossos is colossal. Its focal point is a central courtyard the size of a football field. This arena's purpose might have remained another puzzle, but the Minoans themselves had shown us: Evans found a fresco that depicted a highly risky and unusual sport. It involved a charging aurochs bull—a now-extinct species the size of a rhino, with long, cruel horns—along with three athletes, a man and two women. In the fresco, one woman faced the bull, holding its horns, while the other woman tossed the man, handspring-style, onto the animal's back. It was a crazy activity, but the scene had a lighthearted quality. These people were *playing,* in a don't-try-this-at-home sort of way.

Wandering through Knossos, I was staggered by the sheer amount of stone that had been used to construct it. There were wide stone roads, long stone staircases, walls made of limestone, floors lined with alabaster. Searching for a way to describe what he found, Evans had used the term "palace," though he was far from certain the word summed up Knossos's role. It was a *hub,* that much was clear, with multiple functions. The Minoans had gathered here for events and rituals and celebrations. They'd kept grain, olive oil, and wine in an extensive web of store-rooms. Artists had worked on these grounds: metalsmith-ing, painting, stone cutting, and pottery studios had been excavated. And in a quiet, shaded room, not particularly big or imposing, someone had sat on a carved stone throne with a tall back. Judging from the throne's size, shape, and decoration, researchers believed that someone had been a woman.

Around the corner from this elegant seat, I found the dolphin fresco. The tour groups hadn't descended yet, so for a moment, anyway, I had the place to myself. The dol-phins were located in an area that may have been used for bathing. There were nooks that might have been closets, a lounge area, a sunken basin, and another ancient flush toilet.

The fresco stretched across the main room. Five life-size dolphins swam in profile among schools of fish and bottom-dwelling sea urchins. The dolphins' eyes and markings were painted stylishly and realistically. I leaned forward to examine the painting, feeling a deep sense of happiness.

My thoughts were interrupted by the arrival of an ex-cited group of Germans, led by a woman shouting through a megaphone. Reluctantly I moved on, giving the fresco a final backward glance. I wished I could travel back in time and catch even a glimpse of the people who'd lived here. I have a feeling I would have liked them. More than anything, I wished I could know what it was like to live in a society that loved the ocean—and all its creatures—as much as the Minoans did.

≈≈≈≈≈≈

I was reading on the pebbly beach at Elounda, a town on Crete's northeast coast where I was spending the last few days of my visit. From where I sat I could see Spinalonga, a haunted-looking island fortress about a mile offshore. In the past, it had been used as a prison and a leper colony. I had thought about taking a boat ride over there, but that trip would have to wait. In my pile of Minoan research papers, I'd come across some amazing information. "The picturesque fishing village of Elounda boasts the remains of the Minoan city of Olous," I read. "Folklore suggests that Olous may in fact be the lost city of Atlantis, and when the waters of the bay are calm, it is possible to snorkel over the walls to explore to sunken remains of this ancient site. Swimming here is good—however watch out for sea urchins. Sadly, all that remains on land is a beautiful mosaic floor featuring dolphins frolicking."

I sat up in my beach chair. This was the first time I'd ever heard of Olous. Reading further, I learned that it had been a busy Minoan port. As many as thirty thousand people had once lived there; Olous had a close connection to Knossos. The city's ruins now lay in shallow water, only five miles from my hotel. After the Minoans vanished from Olous, others had moved in, and later inhabitants had minted coins with Britomartis, the mermaid goddess, on one side, and a dolphin on the other. These coins, I read, were now on display in Paris, at the Louvre.

Really? *A sunken Minoan dolphin city? With mermaids?* And it was right here? I gathered my things and ran back to my room. I didn't have a snorkel, but that wasn't going to stop me.

～～～

The directions to Olous were tricky. I drove back through Elounda village, then hung a left at a cobblestone alley. The alley led to a shoreline road that tracked along the water, so low to the sea that a ripple would have swamped it. I knew I was on the right path when I passed the Britomartis Motel, a crummy-looking place that the mermaid goddess would not have enjoyed. Five minutes later I crossed a stone bridge, and then the road ended at the base of some foothills, clumpy with brush. There wasn't much here: a few shanty houses, a shuttered restaurant, some feral cats. Not a person to be seen. I pulled my car onto a patch of dirt, got out, and looked around. The air smelled like salt. All I could hear was the slightest shush of the wind.

I set out to find the dolphin mosaic first, picking my way across a rocky field. There were no signs or guideposts, but there was a trampled footpath, so I followed it, disturbing a herd of goats and a jittery lizard with a mustard-colored head. I hiked past an old boat keeled over in the scrub grass, with snail shells scattered around it. The trail led to a wire fence that enclosed a space the size of a tennis court. In the middle were the dolphins.

Four of them swam across the ruin, escorted by little fish. Somebody must have spent years assembling them, setting thousands of dime-size black and white stones into contrasting patterns. The dolphins were black, with exaggerated white eyes and round black pupils; their beaks were white, with a black outline. Around them, the mosaic exploded into checkerboards, lines, triangles, arches, flowers, shapes that were meant as waves. The center of the floor had been scoured by time, but the dolphins were in excellent shape. They wouldn't last forever, though, because they were totally exposed to the weather.

I lingered for a while and then turned back, anxious to find the sunken city of Olous. It was getting late in the afternoon. The shadows had lengthened, and as I walked, I began to notice something I hadn't seen before: the outlines of buildings. I stopped in my tracks. Earlier, this landscape had seemed empty; now I saw that every hillside was crisscrossed by low stone walls. This *was* a city, but rather than being carefully excavated and protected like Knossos or Akrotiri, it was melting back into the earth.

I followed a wall that led straight into the water, and then stripped down to my bathing suit. Even from above, I could see what lay below the surface. There were ruins down there, vague but unmistakable. As I dropped my clothes on the shore, I realized that shards of pottery were everywhere under my feet. Some of them were even painted. I stepped carefully across the rocks and slipped in.

The sea was aquamarine and as clear as glass. Fish darted around me as I stroked into the bay. The seafloor gradually dropped off. I dove and saw that, on the bottom, algae sprouted between the cracks of stone foundations. Hours passed like minutes as I traced Olous in its aquatic afterlife. Sea urchins guarded doorways; a rainbow-colored eel flashed in the late sunlight of the day. Atlantis this was not, but Olous still made my spirit soar. I swam over to a staircase that led into the depths, and I felt the Minoans beckoning me.

What—and who—was down there? What mysteries

lived beneath the ocean's blue skin? Only the dolphins knew. If there was anything I had learned it was that they, not we, were the masters of their element. Their voices were not ours, their language was unknown to us, but if we listened we could hear their song. It was an ageless, rapturous melody, only faintly heard but somehow known by heart. It echoed through the waters; it rang across the shoals of life.

What if nature spoke to us in music, and the dolphins were her chorus? What if we stopped talking, and joined their harmony?

What if the world was singing to us all the time?

Acknowledgments

Thank you to the many dolphin lovers who helped me during every phase of this book. In the science world, I am indebted to Robin Baird, Daniel Webster, Brenda Rone, and the other scientists at the Cascadia Research Collective. I also owe thanks to Lori Marino, whose work is as inspiring as it is informative. I look forward to following her next project, the Kimmela Center for Animal Advocacy.

During my reporting I was constantly aware of the efforts of individuals and environmental groups to fight necessary battles on behalf of dolphins and whales. In this realm, I am grateful to Ric O'Barry. His devotion to dolphins is legendary, and he has spurred an entire generation of activists. Likewise, I am grateful to the Cove Monitors, everyone who has gone to Taiji to work for a better future there, for dolphins and people.

At Earth Island Institute, Mark Berman, Mark Palmer, and David Phillips provided support and guidance. The ocean has formidable friends in these men. Further thanks go to Frances Beinecke, Joel Reynolds, and Michael Jasny at the Natural Resources Defense Council, and David Henkin at Earthjustice. Both groups work tirelessly—and effectively—to protect the natural world, in times when the stakes have never been higher. Thanks also to Mati Waiya, Luhui'Isha Waiya, and everyone involved with Wishtoyo Chumash Village, a model of environmental stewardship.

No place I traveled to was more inspiring than Thera. The Minoans may be gone, but their stunning artworks remain, so many of them featuring dolphins. For insights into that time and that region, I am grateful to archaeologist Lefteris Zorzos.

At Random House I owe thanks to Beverly Horowitz, for guiding this edition for young readers. Thanks also to my agent, Eric Simonoff, and the team at William Morris Endeavor. Finally, thank you to my family: Bob Casey, Pamela Manning Casey, Sarah Casey, Michael Casey, and Leo and Mia and Rennio, my loves.

Selected Bibliography

Bearzi, Maddalena, and Craig B. Stanford. *Beautiful Minds: The Parallel Lives of Great Apes and Dolphins.* Cambridge, MA: Harvard University Press, 2008.

Caldwell, David K., and Melba C. Caldwell. *The World of the Bottlenosed Dolphin.* Philadelphia: J. B. Lippincott Company, 1972.

Carwardine, Mark. *Whales, Dolphins, and Porpoises.* 2nd ed. New York: Dorling Kindersley Publishing, 2002.

Devine, Eleanore and Martha Clark, eds. *The Dolphin Smile: Twenty-Nine Centuries of Dolphin Lore.* New York: The MacMillan Company, 1967.

Dudzinski, Kathleen M., and Toni Frohoff. *Dolphin Mysteries: Unlocking the Secrets of Communication.* New Haven, CT: Yale University Press, 2008.

Eiseley, Loren. *The Star Thrower.* New York: Harcourt Brace Jovanovich, 1978.

Ellis, Richard. *Dolphins and Porpoises.* New York: Alfred A. Knopf, 1982.

Fichtelius, Karl-Erik, and Sverre Sjolander. *Smarter Than Man? Intelligence in Whales, Dolphins, and Humans.* New York: Pantheon Books, 1972.

Gregg, Justin. *Are Dolphins Really That Smart? The Mammal Behind the Myth.* Oxford: Oxford University Press, 2013.

Hardy, D.A.; C.G. Doumas; J.A. Sakellarakis; and P.M. Warren, eds. *Thera and the Aegean World III: Volume One, Archaeology.* London: The Thera Foundation, 1990.

Herman, Louis M., ed. *Cetacean Behavior: Mechanisms & Functions.* New York: John Wiley & Sons, 1980.

Herzing, Denise L. *Dolphin Diaries: My 25 Years with Spotted Dolphins in the Bahamas.* New York: St. Martin's Press, 2011.

Horwitz, Joshua. *War of the Whales.* New York: Simon & Schuster, 2014.

Jones, Hardy. *The Voice of the Dolphins.* St. Augustine, FL: Bluevoice, 2011.

Kirby, David. *Death at SeaWorld: Shamu and the Dark Side of Killer Whales in Captivity.* New York: St. Martin's Press, 2012.

Mann, Janet; Richard C. Connor; Peter L. Tyack; and Hal Whitehead, eds. *Cetacean Societies: Field Studies of Dolphins and Whales.* Chicago: University of Chicago Press, 2000.

Marinatos, Spyridon. *Life and Art in Prehistoric Thera.* London: Oxford University Press, 1972.

Messinger, Cheryl, and Terran McGinnis. *Marineland.* Charleston, SC: Arcadia Publishing, 2011.

Montagu, Ashley, and John C. Lilly. "The Dolphin in History." Papers delivered by Ashley Montagu and John C. Lilly at a Symposium at the Clark Library, 13 October, 1962.

Norris, Kenneth S. *Dolphin Days: The Life and Times of the Spinner Dolphin.* New York: W.W. Norton & Company, 1991.

Norris, Kenneth S.; Bernd Würsig; Randall S. Wells; and Melany Würsig. *The Hawaiian Spinner Dolphin.* Berkeley, CA: University of California Press, 1994.

O'Barry, Richard, with Keith Coulbourn. *Behind the Dolphin Smile: One Man's Campaign to Protect the World's Dolphins.* Los Angeles: Renaissance Books, 1999.

Ocean, Joan. *Dolphins into the Future.* Kailua, HI: Dolphin Connection, 1997.

Pryor, Karen, and Kenneth S. Norris, eds. *Dolphin Societies: Discoveries and Puzzles.* Berkeley, CA: University of California Press, 1991.

Reiss, Diana. *The Dolphin in the Mirror: Exploring Dolphin Minds and Saving Dolphin Lives.* Boston: Houghton Mifflin Harcourt, 2011.

Schusterman, Ronald J.; Jeanette A. Thomas; and Forrest G. Wood, eds. *Dolphin Cognition and Behavior: A Comparative Approach.* Hillsdale, NJ: Lawrence Erlbaum Associates, 1986.

Scully, Matthew. *Dominion: The Power of Man, the Suffering of Animals, and the Call to Mercy.* New York: St. Martin's Press, 2002.

Smolker, Rachel. *To Touch a Wild Dolphin: A Journey of Discovery with the Sea's Most Intelligent Creatures.* New York: Anchor Books, 2002.

Vougioukalakis, George A. *The Minoan Eruption of the Thera Volcano and the Aegean World.* Athens: Society for the Promotion of Studies on Prehistoric Thera, 2008.

White, Thomas I. *In Defense of Dolphins: The New Moral Frontier.* Malden, MA: Blackwell Publishing, 2007.

Whitehead, Hal, and Luke Rendell. *The Cultural Lives of Whales and Dolphins.* Chicago: University of Chicago Press, 2015.

Videos

Blackfish. Directed by Gabriela Cowperthwaite, produced by Manuel Oteyza and Gabriela Cowperthwaite. CNN Films: July 2013. blackfishmovie.com.

The Cove. Directed by Louis Psihoyos, produced by Paula DuPré Pesman and Fisher Stevens. Participant Media: July 2009. thecovemovie.com.

Scientific and Environmental Resources

BLUE FRONTIER
bluefront.org

CASCADIA RESEARCH
COLLECTIVE
cascadiaresearch.org

CENTER FOR WHALE
RESEARCH
whaleresearch.com

EARTH ISLAND INSTITUTE
earthisland.org

EARTHJUSTICE
earthjustice.org

THE HUMANE SOCIETY OF THE
UNITED STATES
humanesociety.org

THE KIMMELA CENTER FOR
ANIMAL ADVOCACY, INC.
kimmela.org

NATURAL RESOURCES DEFENSE
COUNCIL
nrdc.org

NONHUMAN RIGHTS PROJECT
nonhumanrightsproject.org

OCEANA
oceana.org

RIC O'BARRY'S DOLPHIN
PROJECT
dolphinproject.net

SURFERS FOR CETACEANS
s4cglobal.org

THE SURFRIDER FOUNDATION
surfrider.org

WATERKEEPER ALLIANCE
waterkeeper.org

WHALE TRUST MAUI
whaletrust.org

WISHTOYO FOUNDATION
wishtoyo.org

Photography Credits